Celebrate
the Century ™

A COLLECTION OF
COMMEMORATIVE STAMPS

1930-1939

CELEBRATE
10
THE CENTURY®
PUT YOUR STAMP
ON HISTORY
1900 ▪ 2000

UNITED STATES POSTAL SERVICE®

UNITED STATES
POSTAL SERVICE

POSTMASTER GENERAL
AND CHIEF EXECUTIVE OFFICER
William J. Henderson

CHIEF MARKETING OFFICER
Allen Kane

EXECUTIVE DIRECTOR, STAMP SERVICES
Azeezaly S. Jaffer

MANAGER, STAMP MARKETING
Valoree Vargo

PROJECT MANAGER
Gary A. Thuro Jr.

TIME
LIFE
BOOKS

TIME-LIFE BOOKS IS A DIVISION OF TIME LIFE INC.

TIME-LIFE
CUSTOM PUBLISHING

VICE PRESIDENT AND PUBLISHER
Terry Newell
VICE PRESIDENT OF
NEW BUSINESS DEVELOPMENT
Michael A. Hurley
DIRECTOR OF NEW PRODUCT DEVELOPMENT
Teresa Graham
DIRECTOR OF EDITORIAL DEVELOPMENT
Jennifer Louise Pearce
DIRECTOR OF DESIGN
Christopher M. Register
CUSTOM MARKETING MANAGER
John Charles Loyack

EDITORIAL STAFF FOR
CELEBRATE THE CENTURY

MANAGING EDITOR
Morin Bishop
EDITORS
Sally Guard, John Bolster, Anthony Zumpano
DESIGNERS
Barbara Chilenskas, Jia Baek
WRITERS
Merrell Noden, Eve Peterson, Rachael Nevins
RESEARCHERS
Jenny Douglas, Lauren Cardonsky
PHOTO EDITOR
Bill Broyles

© 1998 UNITED STATES POSTAL SERVICE
All rights reserved.

First printing. Printed in U.S.A.

TIME-LIFE is a trademark of Time Warner Inc. U.S.A.

LIBRARY OF CONGRESS CATALOGING-IN-PUBLICATION DATA
Celebrate the century: a collection of commemorative stamps.
p. cm. Includes index.
Contents: v. 4. 1930–1939
ISBN 0-7835-5320-X
1. Commemorative postage stamps—United States—History—20th century.
2. United States—History—20th century.
I. Time-Life Books
HE6185.U5C45 1998   97–46952
769.56973—DC21   CIP

Books produced by Time-Life Custom Publishing are available at a special bulk discount for promotional and premium use. Custom adaptations can also be created to meet your specific marketing goals. Call 1-800-323-5255.

PICTURE CREDITS

Cover, UPI/Corbis-Bettmann; 4, UPI/Corbis-Bettmann; 5, FDR Library; 6, Underwood Photo Archives, SF; 7, Brown Brothers; 8, New York Times Co./Archive Photos; 9, UPI/Corbis-Bettmann; 10, FDR Library; 11, top, Brown Brothers; 12, top, Corbis; inset, Culver Pictures; 13, left, FDR library; inset, FDR Library; 14, top, FDR Library; inset, FDR Library; 15, FDR Library; 16, Popperfoto/Archive Photos; 17, top, Popperfoto/Archive Photos; 18, Underwood Photo Archives; 19, left, Underwood Photo Archives; right, Archive Photos; 20, top left, Underwood Photo Archives; inset, Underwood Photo Archives; 21, top, Underwood Photo Archives; bottom, UPI/Corbis-Bettmann; 22, Culver Pictures; 23, top, Corbis-Bettmann; 24, top left, FDR Library; bottom left, Archive Photos; right, Archive Photos; 25, Archive Photos; 26, top left, Brown Brothers; top right, Archive Photos; inset, Underwood Photo Archives, SF; 27, Underwood Photo Archives, SF; 28, UPI/Corbis-Bettmann; 29, top, UPI/Corbis-Bettmann; 30, top, UPI/Corbis-Bettmann; bottom, Culver Pictures; 31, left, FDR Library; right, UPI/Corbis-Bettmann; 32, left, Brown Brothers; right, FDR Library; 33, top left, Underwood Photo Archives, SF; top and insets (buttons), Corbis-Bettmann; 34, UPI/Corbis-Bettman; 35, top, Brown Brothers; inset (stamp), "Gone With The Wind"™, its characters and elements are trademarks of Turner Entertainment Co. and the Stephens Mitchell Trusts; 36, left, Archive Photos; right, Photofest; 37, Culver Pictures; 38, AP/Wide World Photos; 39, top, Brown Brothers; inset (stamp), Jesse Owens™ Estate of Jesse Owens c/o CMG Worldwide, Indpl, IN.; 40, left, Popperfoto/Archive Photos; inset, Popperfoto/Archive Photos; 40-41, Popperfoto/Archive Photos; 41, UPI/Corbis-Bettmann; 42, inset, AP/Wide World Photos; 42-43, UPI/Corbis-Bettmann; 43, Ohio State University Archives; 44, DC Comics; 45, top, DC Comics; inset (stamp), SUPERMAN and all related characters, names and indicia are trademarks of DC Comics ©1998. All Rights Reserved. Used with permission; 46, DC Comics; 47, DC Comics; 48, top left, Bill Broyles Collection; bottom left, Bill Broyles Collection; right, DC Comics; 49, left, DC Comics; inset, Geoff Spear/DC Comics; 50, FDR Library; 51, top, FDR Library; 52, top left, National Archives and Records Administration; top right, UPI/Corbis-Bettmann; bottom left, National Archives and Records Administration; bottom right, FDR Library; 53, FDR Library; 54, top, FDR Library; bottom, Library of Congress; 55, top, UPI/Corbis-Bettmann; inset, FDR Library; 56, Margaret Bourke-White/Life; 57, top, UPI/Corbis-Bettmann; inset (stamp), LIFE Magazine ©1936 Time Inc.; 58, Margaret Bourke-White/Life; 59, right, Time Inc. Picture Collection; inset, Margaret Bourke-White/Life; 60, top left, Carl Mydens/Life; top center, Alfred Eisenstaedt/Life; top right, Alfred Eisenstaedt/Life; middle left, Alfred Eisenstaedt/Life; middle right, Dorothea Lange; bottom left, Carl Mydens/Life; bottom center, Margaret Bourke-White/Life; bottom right, Alfred Eisenstaedt/Life; 61, top left, William Vandivert/Life; top center, Margaret Bourke-White/Life; top right, Alfred Eisenstaedt/Life; bottom, Hansel Mieth/Life; 62, UPI/Corbis-Bettmann; 63, top, The *Forbes* Magazine Collection; inset (stamp), MONOPOLY® & ©1998 Hasbro Inc. All Rights Reserved; 64, The *Forbes* Magazine Collection; 65, Parker Brothers; 66, Corbis-Bettmann; 67, top, UPI/Corbis-Bettmann; inset (stamp); 68, top left, FDR Library; top right, UPI/Corbis-Bettmann; bottom, FDR Library; 69, UPI/Corbis-Bettmann; 70, top left, UPI/Corbis-Bettmann; top right, UPI/Corbis-Bettmann; inset, UPI/Corbis-Bettmann; 71, top, FDR Library; bottom, UPI/Corbis-Bettmann; 72, Popperfoto/Archive Photos; 73, top, UPI/Corbis-Bettmann; inset (stamp), The image of Bobby Jones is officially licensed by the heirs of Robert T. ("Bobby") Jones, Jr.; 74, top, UPI/Corbis-Bettmann; bottom, UPI/Corbis-Bettmann; 75, Culver Pictures; 76, top, UPI/Corbis-Bettmann; bottom, UPI/Corbis-Bettmann; 77, top left, Tony Stone/Hulton Getty; top right, UPI/Corbis-Bettmann; bottom right, UPI/Corbis-Bettmann; 78, New York Central System Historical Society; 79, top, Underwood Photo Archives, SF; 80, top, Culver Pictures; inset, Culver Pictures; 81, Archive Photos; 82, top, Tony Stone/ Hulton Getty; bottom left (clock), Cooper-Hewitt, National Design Museum, Smithsonian Institution/ Art Resource, NY, photo: Dennis Cowley; (toaster), Cooper-Hewitt, National Design Museum, Smithsonian Institution/ Art Resource, NY, photo: Dave King; (telephone), Cooper-Hewitt, National Design Museum, Smithsonian Institution/ Art Resource, NY, photo: Dennis Cowley; 83, top, The Metropolitan Museum of Art; bottom, Brown Brothers; 84, Avery Architectural and Fine Arts Library, Columbia University; 85, top, Avery Architectural and Fine Arts Library, Columbia University; 86, top left, Avery Architectural and Fine Arts Library, Columbia University; bottom left, Avery Architectural and Fine Arts Library, Columbia University; inset, Avery Architectural and Fine Arts Library, Columbia University; 87, UPI/Corbis-Bettman; 88, top left, Archive Photos; top right, Archive Photos; inset, Corbis-Bettmann; 89, UPI/Corbis-Bettmann; 90, Collection of Steve and Nancy Ison; 91, Collection of Steve and Nancy Ison; 92, top, ©Disney; insets, ©Disney; bottom, Collection of Steve and Nancy Ison; 93, top, Collection of Steve and Nancy Ison; inset, Collection of Steve and Nancy Ison; 94, left, Collection of Steve and Nancy Ison; top right, ©Disney; bottom right, ©Disney; 95, top, Collection of Steve and Nancy Ison; insets, ©Disney.

CONTENTS

Roosevelt (opposite page) offered calm confidence to a nation shaken by the ravages of the Depression (above).

INTRODUCTION

In December 1930, slightly more than a year after the stock market crash, President Herbert Hoover assured Congress that "the fundamental strength of the economy is unimpaired." A short time later Hoover responded to a question about the prevalence of street-corner apple salesmen—jobless men who purchased surplus apples on credit to resell them at a nickel each—by saying, "Many people have left their jobs for the more profitable one of selling apples." In 1932 Hoover told the writer Christopher Morley, "What this country needs is a great poem;" and in the spring of that year the President urged crooner Rudy Vallee to "sing a song that would make people forget the Depression." But such a song did not exist; instead, Vallee sang one that went like this:

They used to tell me I was building a dream
And so I followed the mob.
When there was earth to plough or guns to bear
I was always right there on the job.

Once I built a railroad, made it run
Made it race against time.
Once I built a railroad, now it's done.
Brother, can you spare a dime?

So began the 1930s—with an embattled President attempting to soothe a suffering, struggling populace whose disenchantment was rapidly descending into hostility. The dizzy excesses of the '20s were a distant memory. Indeed, no two consecutive decades in the twentieth century were more starkly opposed than the '20s and the '30s.

5

The Golden Gate Bridge was a stirring symbol of American perseverance and ingenuity.

The '20s bubbled over with gin mills, flappers and the Charleston, while the '30s were a parched procession of bread lines, drought-blighted farms and men who viewed jail time, with its shelter and three meals a day, as a blessing. This was the decade in which the word 'unemployed' became a noun in addition to an adjective. The newspaperman who had coined the 1928 Republican campaign slogan, "A chicken in every pot and two cars in every garage," was broke by 1933 and seeking loans to support his family. The United States came to question its most fundamental assumptions about democracy and the American Dream.

When times were at their worst there was more than a whiff of revolution in the air. Those on the left of the political spectrum leaned toward Communism as the solution, while those on the right inched toward totalitarianism. Republican Senator David A. Reed said in 1932, "If this country ever needed a Mussolini, it needs one now." There was no lack of precedent, either: Seven countries in Latin America had been moved to revolution by economic depressions less severe than the one the United States was enduring.

But the foundation would hold, and so the '30s were about rebirth as much as they were about hard times. This was the era of Franklin Delano Roosevelt and the New Deal, beacons of hope in the gloomy early years of the decade. "Happy Days Are Here Again" was the official song of the 1932 Roosevelt presidential campaign, and while that wasn't strictly true, the prospect of happy days, at least, had returned.

Despite the stalled economy, marvels of engineering such as the Golden Gate Bridge and the Empire State Building rose on both coasts. National landmarks, they stand as symbols of America's perseverance and ingenuity in the face of adversity. A people struggling to overcome hard times raised its eyes to heroes like Jesse Owens, who streaked through the center of the decade, the perfect foil for Hitler's villainy, and Bobby Jones, the elegant golfer who in 1930 completed the only Grand Slam in the history of the sport. The White House was home to two heroes, for Roosevelt's wife, Eleanor, gracefully complemented and extended his leadership, redefining the role of First Lady.

America also found relief in imaginary heroes. Superman made his comic book debut in June 1938 and he too was an instant success. Soon he would be vanquishing Nazis. The board game *Monopoly* offered a fantasy antidote to the economic crisis; playing the game, down-on-their-luck Americans could be J. P. Morgans and Andrew Mellons for a few heady hours. Romantic epics like Margaret Mitchell's *Gone With the Wind*, with its determined heroine, Scarlett O'Hara, offered escapist glimpses of another difficult period of rebuilding, the Civil War Reconstruction era.

The 1939 New York World's Fair would close the decade, and its theme of "Building the World of Tomorrow," exemplified the growing mood of optimism in the country. A new style of design, the streamlined look, was in vogue, and it permeated the Fair. With its modern, curvilinear forms, the style seemed to herald a bright shining future.

The rising tide of optimism, however, would be tempered with melancholy as war broke out abroad. America had progressed from the rambunctious adolescence of the '20s to a cautious maturity by the end of the '30s. She was waxing again, but remained guarded.

By the time Hoover made his 1932 comment about the apple salesmen, his denial of the country's dire straits had reached comic depths, and the backlash against him turned lethal. Sprawling shantytowns of tarpaper shacks scattered across the country were dubbed Hoovervilles. New York had two massive Hoovervilles, one in Central Park, the other below Riverside Drive. Newspapers that the homeless used to cover themselves as they slept on park benches were known as Hoover blankets, and empty pockets, turned inside out, were Hoover flags.

Nineteen-thirty-two was the nadir for both the country and the Hoover administration. He hit rock bottom on July 28, when he loosed the U.S.

Heroes such as Owens (above) were a needed salve for troubled times.

Army on thousands of World War veterans, so-called bonus marchers who had gathered peacefully all summer near the Capitol seeking early payment of their soldiers' bonuses to counteract their economic hardship. Many of those veterans had wives and children in tow.

Led by General Douglas MacArthur and Major George S. Patton Jr., several divisions of the Army routed the unarmed vets and their families with tear gas and bayonets, chasing them back to their headquarters along the Anacostia River. Two veterans and one infant were killed and hundreds were wounded in the confrontation, which ended with the Army's burning the marchers' encampment.

This was the political death knell for Hoover, who, while steadfastly refusing to enact federal relief for the ailing economy, had established the Reconstruction Finance Corporation (RFC) to support failing banks. Many denounced the RFC as a "bread line for big business." Indeed, its first president, Chicago banker Charles Dawes, loaned $90 million to his own bank soon after taking over the bureau. A popular joke held that Hoover asked the Secretary of the Treasury for a nickel to call a friend and the Secretary replied, "Here's a dime, phone both of them."

Hoover nevertheless won the Republican nomination in 1932 and, amazingly, was considered the favorite in the early part of the campaign. That was before Roosevelt's pledge of a "New Deal for the American people" had taken hold. His silver-

Labor-saving gadgets became a staple in more and more home in the '30s.

spoon background notwithstanding, Roosevelt genuinely empathized with the down-and-out and the voters sensed it. Traversing the Great Plains on the campaign trail that year, Roosevelt saw firsthand the ravages of the Depression. "I have looked into the faces of thousands of Americans," he told a friend. "They have the frightened look of lost children."

The dispossessed he encountered were not career hobos (though there were plenty of those); rather, they came from every sector of society, many of them from the middle class. Cleveland Mayor Newton D. Baker wrote in *The New York Times* that they ranged, "from the college graduate to the child who has never seen the inside of the schoolhouse. Expectant mothers, sick babies, young childless couples, grim-faced middle-aged dislodged from lifetime jobs—on they go, an in-

dex of insecurity…. We think of nomads of the desert—now we have nomads of the Depression." They responded to Roosevelt as though reunited with a long-lost father. He won the 1932 election by the largest margin in a two-party presidential race since Abraham Lincoln trounced George McClellan in 1864. Roosevelt carried 42 of the 48 states and won 472 electoral votes to Hoover's 59.

The new President wasted no time addressing the nation's woes, creating an emergency banking bill on his very first day in office. Within 100 days he had signed 15 significant bills into law. Roosevelt believed that the government bore a responsibility for the welfare of its people, and his New Deal was composed of a series of programs and commissions intended to boost the nation's lot. Many of the programs, including the Federal Deposit Insurance Corporation, the Tennessee Valley Authority and the Securities Exchange Commission, endure today. Perhaps the greatest symbol of Roosevelt's political values, and his self-described crowning achievement, was the Social Security Act of 1935. This legislation provided a safety net for the elderly, the infirm and the unemployed.

The New Deal was not without its critics, especially within big business, and it was by no means a magic panacea. But by the middle of the decade the economy was showing signs of recovery. In 1936 unemployment was less than half of what it had been in '32. Industrial production had more than doubled, and incomes and company profits had increased by more than 50 percent.

People could now forget their cares, if only fleetingly. There was room in life again for entertainment. Fred Astaire and Ginger Rogers waltzed into the nation's consciousness via the silver screen, to which 85 million Americans flocked weekly, an enormous figure given the economic

A visit by Roosevelt (center) in 1933 gave these Civilian Conservation Corps workers an opportunity to voice their wholehearted support for the New Deal and for the president who created it.

climate of the times. A twist of the radio dial yielded Jack Benny or *The Lone Ranger*, while Dick Tracy kept order in the Sunday funnies. Swing was the latest musical craze, practiced most notably—at least in white society—by Benny Goodman. The seeds of the electronics industry began to sprout in the mid-'30s, as labor-saving gadgets cropped up in more and more homes; and in 1936 RCA authorized the first field testing of a technology called television, which would add pictures to radio. *Life* magazine debuted in November of that year with an optimistic mission statement that read in part, "to see and take pleasure in seeing; to see and be amazed; to see and be instructed."

The election of 1936 would amount to the nation's evaluation of Roosevelt's New Deal. Times were still tough, certainly, but Americans showed overwhelmingly that they believed things were getting better: Roosevelt won the largest landslide in U.S. history, taking 523 electoral votes to Republican Alf Landon's eight; Landon won only two states, Maine and Vermont. In a quip typical of his jousting style with the press, Roosevelt told White House reporters, "I knew I should have gone to Maine and Vermont, but Jim [Roosevelt's son] wouldn't let me."

The last piece of New Deal legislation, the Fair Labor Standards Act, completed its journey through Congress in June 1938. In the fall the GOP would rebound in Congress and Roosevelt's legislative flurry would abate. The country had largely put its house in order, but in its preoccupation with domestic affairs had ignored its next challenges, ominously assembling in Germany and Japan.

THE DEPRESSION

The Great Crash, it turned out, was only the first blow. Thousands of Americans lost their fortunes in the stock market collapse of October 1929, but that catastrophe merely triggered a cycle in which industry cutbacks led to unemployment, which in turn led to more industry cutbacks because workers who had no income could not buy industrial goods. By 1933 nearly 13 million people—about 25 percent of the national work force—were unemployed. For seven of the next eight years the average number of unemployed workers remained at or above eight million. Whereas through the 1920s confidence in the economy had risen in a delirium out of proportion with the economy's real growth, in the first three years of the '30s, faced with closed banks and factories, sun-scorched farms, and hungry families, Americans' confidence plummeted as precipitously as the stock market had.

While the declines of financial empires captured headlines, those most crushed by the rapidly imploding economy were small farmers and laborers who had long struggled on the brink of poverty and, of course, had had nothing to do with the wild speculation of the '20s. "There is not an unemployed man in the country that hasn't contributed to the wealth of every millionaire in America," said humorist and social commentator Will Rogers, voicing the thoughts of the millions who found themselves waiting in lines for handouts of soup and bread. "The working classes didn't bring this on, it was the big boys that thought the financial drunk was going to last forever."

Many who lost their homes, unable to pay rent, took up residence in shantytowns that sprung up on empty lots, by riverbanks, and even in city dumps. They called their new abodes "Hoover-

With unemployment at staggering levels, many Americans lined up for handouts (above), while others lost hope (left).

"We do not dare to use even a little soap when it will pay for an extra egg or a few more carrots for our children."

—*A LETTER TO THE WHITE HOUSE, EARLY 1930s*

Two essentials—food and shelter—became out of reach for millions of Americans, many of whom were forced to dwell in "Hoovervilles" (opposite page) and rely on soup lines (above, right) and subsidized meals (above).

villes," after the sitting president whose policies seemed incapable of stabilizing the economy, let alone helping them feed their children.

Mid- and southwestern farmers already suffering from a sharp decline in prices saw the very heavens and earth turn against them in the early '30s. Drought scorched the Great Plains from Texas to South Dakota, and in a section of the wheat belt that covered parts of Colorado, Kansas, New Mexico, Oklahoma and Texas, soil that had already been weakened by overcultivation yielded to the wind. Thousands upon thousands of acres of topsoil were thrown into the air in stunning, devastating dust storms that sometimes drifted as far east as New England and the Atlantic Coast.

Had the American Dream proved to be an illusion? The blighted heartland seemed to say so. And yet thousands of southwesterners—known as Dust Bowl refugees and "Okies" even though many of them came from neither the Dust Bowl nor Oklahoma—abandoned their homes for the promised land of California, demonstrating their unswerving belief in the westward movement that had played such a vital part in the American story. For many the promise of the West proved more than symbolic; the Depression had hit California as hard as it

13

Parts of rural America were decimated as dust storms left once-fertile land unusable (above) and prompted countless Americans to undertake cross-country treks (opposite page); Lange's photographs recorded the quiet dignity of the "Okies" (right).

had any other state, but by 1933 California's economy began to grow steadily, giving rise to new jobs, particularly in agriculture. Still, unemployment in that state remained high through the '30s, and many southwesterners arrived there to find no more opportunities than there were at home.

To artists and intellectuals, such as novelist John Steinbeck and photographer Dorothea Lange, these displaced people embodied the challenge the

14

Depression posed to the ideal of the United States as a land of opportunity. Even while documenting the suffering of Americans, though, Steinbeck, in *The Grapes of Wrath*, and Lange, in her images of lined faces and level gazes, both presented a message of hope by revealing, as Lange said, their subjects' "real courage. Undeniable courage."

Armed with that courage and with a belief in change and innovation, Americans in 1932 rejected the old ideas represented by Herbert Hoover in favor of the "New Deal" proposed by Franklin Delano Roosevelt, who promised that his government would take an active role in righting the nation's economy. The ensuing years would vindicate their judgment.

Aftermath

The United States enjoyed unprecedented prosperity in the two decades following World War II. The regulatory laws and institutions established in the New Deal, however, have not completely insulated the national economy from the fluctuations inherent in capitalism. The energy crisis of the 1970s, which exposed the dangers of American dependence on a limited resource, brought on high inflation and unemployment.

After an economic boom in the '80s, another recession slowed the economy in the early '90s, ending in 1994, when a bull market began its rampage through the record books.

THE GOLDEN GATE BRIDGE

On a business trip to San Francisco in August 1916, Chicago-based engineer Joseph Baerman Strauss came across an article in the San Francisco *Call-Bulletin* that intrigued him. In it, an engineer named James Wilkins proposed that a bridge be built across the Golden Gate, the mile-wide corridor of water that links San Francisco Bay to the Pacific Ocean. Some 20 years later, Strauss would realize Wilkins's dream.

During his 47-year career Strauss would build more than 400 bridges throughout the world, but here he conceived his crowning glory. A bridge across the Golden Gate would be the longest in the world, and overcoming the obstacles to its construction would be an unprecedented feat.

Talk about a bridge over troubled water: The Golden Gate is more than 380 feet deep in places, and powerful winds regularly whip through the channel. Ocean-scale waves and currents, sucked in by the expansive San Francisco Bay, are common,

and winter storms from the Pacific pound the coast. Topping all of that off is the very real threat of an earthquake.

San Francisco had only recently recovered from the devastating 1906 quake and fire that killed thousands of people and left more than 200,000 homeless. The man in charge of the city's rebuilding effort, Michael O'Shaughnessy, believed that connecting San Francisco to the Marin County communities on the north side of the bay would bolster the city's growth and prosperity. But every engineer he talked to told him either that the bridge could not be built or that it would cost a prohibitive $100 million. When O'Shaughnessy consulted Strauss in 1919, however, Strauss said he could build the bridge at a cost of $25 million. Strauss contended, as Wilkins had, that a suspension bridge—in which the weight of the roadway is supported by cables suspended from above—would be the only viable design.

Ineffably elegant, the Golden Gate Bridge (opposite page and above) also served a viable economic purpose.

"A giant portal that seems like a mighty door, swinging wide into a world of wonders."

—Joseph Strauss, in his dedication speech, February 25, 1933

While the construction of the massive towers (opposite page) may have been the most impressive engineering feat, Strauss's ingenuity also shone through in the system of catwalks (above), which gave workers the footing needed to hang the cables (left) from which the roadway was suspended.

The next step, gaining approval for the project, proved to be nearly as challenging as the actual construction would. Strauss and O'Shaughnessy endured an 13-year political and fund-raising odyssey and weathered 2,000 lawsuits from groups opposed to the bridge before they began construction. Finally, on February 26, 1933, Strauss's company officially broke ground. An estimated 200,000 people attended the ceremony.

The construction of the bridge was replete with engineering challenges, most notably in the laying of the foundations for the bridge's two towers. The south tower had to be plunged into the bedrock 1,125 feet from shore, where the turbulent water was 60 feet deep. For this purpose a cofferdam—a watertight enclosure—and an elevated road leading to it were built. Once the cofferdam was pumped free of water, the men had a clear space in which to work, as well as a veritable banquet of flopping, scurrying seafood, which they collected and brought home to their families.

As fiercely determined as Strauss was to complete the project, he never compromised the safety of his workers. In fact he introduced a number of precautions that have become industry standards. Foremost among these was the use of huge nets strung 10 feet below the roadway. Nineteen men—the self-described "Halfway to Hell Club"—fell into these

When the workers finished stringing and reinforcing the cables (above and inset), they began the most dangerous part of the undertaking, putting the roadway in place (opposite page, above); upon completion of the bridge on May 27, 1937, pedestrians jubilantly streamed across its span (opposite page, below).

during the 11 months in which the road was built. Through the first three and a half years none died—an amazing record given the average in that era of one death per every million dollars spent on a project. Sadly, two fatal accidents did occur during the final stages of the job. On October 21, 1936, one man fell to his death, and on February 17, 1937, just months from the completion date, a scaffold holding 12 men detached from the roadway, tore through the safety net and plummeted into the channel. Ten of the men were killed. A plaque near the San Francisco side of the bridge honors their memory.

With the bridge nearing completion, architect Irving Morrow added the final touch, the striking International Orange hue. Morrow conducted a series of tests in the salt air of the Golden Gate before making his choice, basing it on the paint's durability, its visibility to ships and the way the color blended with the hills of Marin County. On May 27, 1937, the bridge opened to pedestrians, and more than 200,000 people paid a nickel each to stroll across the majestic span.

Aftermath

The Golden Gate Bridge remains a national landmark as well as a marvel of engineering, but it has required some alterations. In 1954, bracing was added to strengthen the roadway, and in 1985, the entire roadbed was replaced. The bridge was completely repainted over a 30-year period beginning in 1965, and touch-up painting remains the primary maintenance task.

Strauss, whose company was paid $1 million for its work, did not see any of these changes, nor did he have long to enjoy his achievement: he died on May 16, 1938.

The Golden Gate Bridge was surpassed as the longest single-span suspension bridge in the world on November 21, 1964, when New York City's Verrazano-Narrows Bridge opened. The distinction now belongs to England's Humber Bridge, which was completed in 1981.

HOUSEHOLD CONVENIENCES

Not so long ago, Americans lived by the rhythm of the changing seasons and the rising and setting sun. Each household was an industry unto itself, usually headed by a genuine partnership of husband and wife. On washday women gathered around the well and clotheslines; they spent afternoons in sewing circles and quilting bees exchanging ideas and techniques. With the coming of winter, men chopped wood and women canned the fall harvest of vegetables. In the spring, houses were turned inside out for annual cleaning. Of course there were also those families with domestic servants to tend the fire and beat the rugs; laundry services to take care of the washing; and governesses to rear the children.

Then came the industrial revolution and urbanization, which by the turn of the century sent hordes of men and domestic servants alike to work in factories. The result? The emergence of the uniquely female occupation of homemaker— a role that would be shaped in large part by the arrival of gas and electric service to urban homes. The electrical industry, eager to boost energy consumption, ushered homemaking into the modern era by developing and marketing drudgery-saving appliances ranging from electric irons and vacuum cleaners to washing machines and stoves. The industry also introduced the egg cooker, the coffee maker and the waffle iron, specifically to increase the need for power during low-use morning hours.

In the century's first two decades, electric helpers were affordable only to upper-class women, many of whom purchased them in an effort to prevent their live-in help from defecting to factories that offered shorter hours and more freedom, if less pay. As electric service expanded and the demand for appliances increased in the 1930s, the prices of both eased. Homemakers of the growing middle class who

The dishwasher (opposite page) was one of the appliances that transformed the traditional kitchen of the '20s (above).

could not afford big-ticket items like refrigerators could nonetheless save time and boost their status by purchasing irons, vacuum cleaners and toasters.

Companies that formerly made farm implements (Maytag), leather goods (Hoover) and shearing clippers (Sunbeam) retooled and began preaching the benefits of efficiency and good hygiene their appliances could provide. Product advertisements featured well-dressed, smiling women who made it seem, for example, that with the flick of a switch, rugs would vacuum them-

selves—a quantum leap from the arduous task of dragging carpets outside and pounding them.

Advertisements for the Sunbeam Mixmaster tacitly promised that the product would elevate the housewife's tasks to a science by making "every cook a better cook" and mixing "every atom thoroughly." More than 60,000 Mixmasters were sold when the product was introduced in 1930, and by 1936, despite the Depression, annual sales had reached 300,000. But just as the Mixmaster's array of attachments enabled it to mix, beat, whip,

"The myth of the 'new woman,' freed by domestic appliances was, essentially, created by advertisers in the inter-war period as a means of selling new appliances."

—*PENNY SPARKE, author, senior tutor at the Royal College of Art, 1987*

While new appliances such as the vacuum cleaner (left), the refrigerator (opposite page, below left and below right) and the washing machine (opposite page, below center and right) required less physical labor than in the dark old days of hand wringers (opposite page, above left), they added to a woman's household chores by making it easier to perform them more often.

25

The New Way
To Cook with..

Built-In ROASTER
IT COOKS · ROASTS · BAKES

WHOLE DINNERS
Cooked Together

If it's a Roaster Range IT'S A
MONARCH

The incessant pitches for new appliances such as stoves (left) and vacuum cleaners (opposite page) helped create an idealized image of the happy home-maker (above, left) with her fully equipped and properly appointed kitchen (above), which every woman was urged to spend the family's hard-earned dollars to create.

grind, chop, juice fruits, open cans and sharpen knives, so the housewife with her new appliances was suddenly expected to do more, and to do it better than before.

Much of the work was significantly easier, but with the growing national obsession with hygiene that appliances fostered, there was more of it. Take laundry. Washday, or Blue Monday, historically had been the most dreaded day in a woman's weekly cycle of chores. Although clothes were worn several times before each washing, laundry was still a time-consuming and physically exhausting task. Women with any discretionary in-

come at all sent clothes to commercial laundries or paid washerwomen to assume at least part of the load.

By the beginning of the '30s more than a quarter of nonfarm households with electricity were equipped with washing machines. Even so, a woman had to fill the machine with water, start it, add soap to it, empty it of water, fill it again, empty it again and run the clothes through the wringer by hand.

Machines did make washing easier, but they also brought the time-consuming chore back into the home and encouraged more frequent washings. By the time fully-automatic washers with spin-dry capability became available in the '40s, the ever-increasing laundry pile was well on its way to becoming a daily burden.

But if women were doing the wash more often, they were shopping for food less frequently—at least in the 56 percent of American households that owned refrigerators by 1940. Improved refrigeration and the concomitant development of frozen foods liberated women from having to shop daily.

The unforeseen effect of all these time- and effort-saving conveniences, however, was that women, who just a few decades earlier might have met at the shared clothesline, the well, the sewing circle, the butcher shop or the commercial laundry, increasingly found themselves at home in the company of their electric helpers, free to do laundry at midnight or chase dust bunnies till dawn.

Aftermath

According to research by sociologist Joann Vanek, full-time housewives in 1924 devoted some 52 hours a week to household chores. In 1966 their counterparts devoted 55—evidence, perhaps, of the joys of homemaking. But consider this: The housewife who in 1928 spent six hours a week doing laundry without the benefit of fully automatic washing machines spent seven hours at the task in 1953, despite the ubiquity of automatic machines. Now, with more women than ever working outside the home, there is evidence that standards of housekeeping are slipping, or at least relinquishing some power. Nonetheless, top-of-the-line appliances, such as Miele vacuum cleaners, Viking ranges and Sub-Zero refrigerators, are highly popular status symbols.

FRANKLIN DELANO ROOSEVELT

If to prove themselves great leaders require great challenges, then Franklin Delano Roosevelt had a doozy of an opportunity when he was sworn in as the 32nd president of the United States on March 4, 1933. The country was in the throes of the Depression. More than 15 million Americans were out of work, and that very morning the nation's few surviving banks had closed their doors. The American people had all but given up, numbed by an economic catastrophe that seemed to challenge the very notion of unfettered free enterprise.

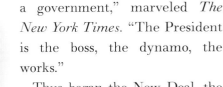

But unlike his predecessor, Herbert Hoover, who had seemed paralyzed by the problems multiplying around him, Roosevelt appeared to relish the challenge that faced him, and he threw himself into his work with unflagging energy and confidence. His first act, on his first day in office, was to create an emergency banking bill, which sailed unaltered through Congress in 38 minutes. "Never was there such a change in the transfer of a government," marveled *The New York Times.* "The President is the boss, the dynamo, the works."

Thus began the New Deal, the most sweeping social and economic program the United States has ever seen. Within 100 days Roosevelt used his apparently bottomless store of intelligence and chutzpah to push 15 major pieces of social and economic legislation through Congress.

Roosevelt's guiding belief was that government bore a fundamental responsibility for the people's happiness, welfare and dignity and should work to promote them. "There's no reason why everybody in the United States should not be covered from the cradle to the grave," he said in describing what he

Roosevelt's common touch, in person (opposite page) and on the radio (above), belied his privileged upbringing.

regarded as the supreme achievement of his administration, the Social Security Act of 1935, which authorized welfare payments and created insurance for the aged, the unemployed and the disabled.

Roosevelt's activism infuriated titans of business: J. P. Morgan forbade the mere mention of Roosevelt's name in his house. Though Roosevelt is still vilified in some quarters as the father of big government, it should be noted that he did not believe in handouts, which he distrusted as "a narcotic, a subtle destroyer of the human spirt," choosing instead to put people to work in meaningful jobs.

Roosevelt was a man of many paradoxes. Though he was born to a world of nannies and silver tea trays, educated at Groton and Harvard, he had a Robin Hood's sympathy for the struggles of ordinary folk. Stricken with polio in 1921 and forced to use crutches or a wheelchair, he was the embodiment of unyielding strength to a nation that had lost its will. "We have nothing to fear but fear itself," he told the country in his first inaugural speech.

Americans responded to Roosevelt's ebullient optimism by giving him their devotion on a scale unprecedented in U.S. political history. Millions

Roosevelt was a brilliant campaigner, whether on the stump as the Democrats' vice-presidential candidate in 1920 (opposite page, below) or as a presidential candidate aboard his *Roosevelt Special* (opposite page, above); Roosevelt had a great affinity for children (left), in part perhaps as a result of the humanizing effects of his disability; swimming, FDR's most frequent form of exercise (below), enabled him to keep his upper body strong.

tuned in to their radios each week to hear his reassuring voice during his "fireside chats," and when he told his listeners there was no problem too large for American ingenuity to overcome, they believed him.

Recent presidents might take a lesson from Roosevelt's confident handling of the press. He actually seemed to enjoy the give and take of press conferences, engaging reporters in debates that were frank and fearless. And newsmen, in what now seems a gesture of extraordinary sensitivity, agreed tacitly never to picture him in his wheelchair or trying to stand.

Roosevelt believed that his disability was the source of his strength. "If you've spent two years in bed trying to wiggle your big toe," he said, "everything else seems easy."

"The test of our progress is not whether we add more to the abundance of those who have much; it is whether we provide enough for those who have too little."
—*FRANKLIN DELANO ROOSEVELT, 1937*

Life had indeed seemed easy for Roosevelt as a young man. Born on January 30, 1882, he grew up on a large estate in Hyde Park, New York, and at age 23 married a distant cousin, Eleanor Roosevelt, who would expand the role of First Lady as much as he did that of president. He began his political career in 1910 as a New York state representative, and would go on to hold a variety of public offices, from assistant secretary of the navy (1913–20) to governor of New York (1929–33). In 1920 he was the Democratic nominee for vice president. When he contracted polio the following year, everyone thought his political career was over. As his subsequent four terms as president would prove, they had greatly underestimated the man.

Though Roosevelt hoped all along that the United States would not have to enter World War II, that dream was dashed when Japan bombed Pearl Harbor on December 7, 1941. Ironically, it was war that dragged the country out of the Depression for good.

But the stress of leading a country in combat took a terrible toll on Roosevelt's health. When he died of a stroke on April 12, 1945, four months before the end of the war, the nation mourned the loss of America's most towering and beloved twentieth century political figure. It's no wonder that historians, in the most recent ranking of U.S. presidents in *The New York Times Sunday Magazine*, placed Roosevelt in the highest echelon, in the company of only Washington and Lincoln.

Roosevelt's jaunty spirit and boundless optimism were irresistible throughout his four presidential campaigns, including his first, in 1932, with John Garner (below, left), which promised an end to the Depression and the repeal of Prohibition.

Aftermath

Barring further amendment to the U.S. Constitution, no one will ever match Franklin Delano Roosevelt's run of four straight terms as president. On February 27, 1951, Congress ratified the 22nd Amendment, which states that "no person shall be elected to the office of the President more than twice, and no person who has held the office of President, or acted as President, for more than two years of a term to which some other person was elected President shall be elected to the office of the President more than once."

Harry Truman, who had succeeded Roosevelt upon his death, was exempted from these conditions and probably could have won a third term. But Truman chose not to run when he sensed public opinion was against his doing so.

The Republicans, who pushed the amendment through, must have been kicking themselves in 1960 when Dwight D. Eisenhower was prevented from entering an election for a third term that he probably could have won.

GONE WITH THE WIND

"No one has read it except her husband, but if she can write the way she talks, it should be a honey of a book." So said editor Lois Cole to her boss, Harold Latham, a senior editor at the Macmillan Publishing Company, hoping that during his 1935 search for writing by new southern authors he might extract the manuscript of the suspected "honey" from its stubborn author, her friend Margaret Mitchell.

Nine years earlier, Mitchell had found herself stuck with a lame ankle in the tiny Atlanta apartment she and her husband, John Marsh, a publicity director at Georgia Power, had named "The Dump." Having been forced to quit her job as a reporter at the same newspaper and having read nearly every book in Atlanta's Carnegie Library, she dedicated herself to writing what her friends teasingly called "the Great American Novel." Mitchell herself called the book "lousy," tucking its

chapters into manila envelopes as she finished them and hiding the envelopes in closets and under chairs, sofa cushions, and her bed.

When Latham arrived in Atlanta in April 1935, Mitchell graciously showed him around town while denying again and again that she had any manuscript for him. Only the taunt of a young writer who was courting Latham's attentions goaded Mitchell into action. Hearing that Mitchell hadn't given Latham her manuscript, the cad said, "My book is grand. Everybody says it'll win the Pulitzer Prize. But, Peggy, I think you are wasting your time trying. You aren't really the type."

Furious, Mitchell surrendered her work—except for the chapters under the bed, which in her anger she forgot—to Latham just before he boarded a train to South Carolina. The next day she sent him a telegram: "Send it back, I've changed my mind." The telegram arrived too

"Lousy" was the early assessment by Mitchell (opposite page) of the bestseller that spawned the blockbuster movie (above).

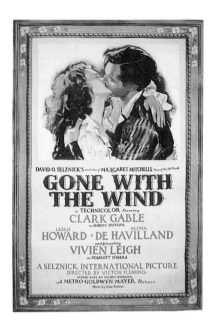

Posters (above) trumpeted the adaptation of Mitchell's classic; the film premiered on December 15, 1939, in Atlanta (right); Hattie Mc-Daniel (opposite page, right, with Vivien Leigh) portrayed one of the African-American characters considered objectionable by civil rights activists.

"**How could I help caring for you—you who have all the passion for life that I have not?...Why you are as elemental as fire and wind and wild things...**"

—*ASHLEY WILKES, to Scarlett O'Hara*

late; Latham already planned to publish what, after six months of revision and scrupulous fact-checking, would become an instant and enduring bestseller and Pulitzer Prize-winning *Gone With the Wind*.

According to some estimates, only the Bible has sold more copies than *Gone With the Wind*. After all, who could fail to love the novel's magnifi-

cently flawed heroine, Scarlett O'Hara, who, in her vanity, greed and ignorance, believes she can grasp whatever she wants, whether it be riches, a man's heart, or her beloved estate, Tara? Who could fail to love the novel's hero, Rhett Butler, "a man of lusty and unashamed appetites," as pragmatic and unconventional as Scarlett but far more sensitive than she? And who isn't crushed to see

Scarlett realize much too late that for 12 years she has pursued the wrong man, that she truly loves Rhett, her estranged husband, who unfortunately no longer gives a damn?

Mitchell's vision of the novel actually began with the scene of Scarlett's final frustration, for Mitchell wrote the last chapter first and worked her way backward through the story. To those who hoped for a happier ending, she conceded only the ambiguous promise of Scarlett's famous words, "Tomorrow, I'll think of some way to get him back. After all, tomorrow is another day." Readers suffering the hunger and loss of the Depression readily identified with Scarlett's determination to overcome the ravages of the Civil War; and, seeing her resourceful—although unprincipled—manipulations yield prosperity, they could hardly doubt that she would get her man back.

Ambiguous outcome or not, America fell for Scarlett's story; within the first six months of publication the novel sold more than a million copies, and Mitchell sold the movie rights to producer David O. Selznick for the unprecedented sum of $50,000. To Mitchell's dismay, his Academy Award-winning 1939 film presented the antebellum South as a world of sweeping, wealthy plantations lorded over by a chivalric white aristocracy. This vision of the South had more to do with Hollywood's romanticism than it did with either the region's history or Mitchell's novel, which she populated with backwoods hunters, swamp trappers, small farmers and planters such as Scarlett's father, Gerald O'Hara, a very successful, somewhat ignorant and hardly genteel Irish immigrant. In the book Tara is no columned mansion but a rambling house of whitewashed brick.

Such differences fade into significance, however, when measured against the one element that forms the core of both works: the passions of Scarlett and Rhett, whose tortured relationship continues to fire the popular imagination.

Aftermath

Not only did Mitchell never write another novel, but she refused to respond to that urgent question: Does Scarlett find a way to get Rhett back? In 1986, the trustee of trusts created by Mitchell's brother Stephens, for the benefit of her two nephews, commissioned Alexandra Ripley, a historical romance writer, to pen the answer to this question. Released in 1991, *Scarlett* spent 48 weeks on the bestseller lists, but will never approach the popularity of *Gone With the Wind*, of which many thousands of copies in more than 40 languages are sold every year.

JESSE OWENS

Carried to empyrean heights by both his own tremendous talent and historical forces far beyond his control, Jesse Owens stands alone as the greatest of Olympic heroes. At the 1936 Games in Berlin, Owens won gold medals in the 100- and 200-meter dashes, the long jump and the 4 x 100-meter relay, in which he led off the world-record-breaking U.S. team. Owens won all of those events by sizable margins, and as sportswriter Grantland Rice saw it, on his final attempt in the long jump Owens looked as if he were leaping "clear out of Germany." Of Owens's Olympic-record run in the 200, Arthur Daley of *The New York Times* wrote, "It was one of the most amazing achievements in the ancient art of foot racing. No one in history had broken even 21 seconds flat for the distance around a turn and here was this human bullet ripping off 0:20.7, his 11th record of one description or another in 14 appearances."

As impressive as Owens was in Berlin, he was helped into the realm of myth by an unlikely source—German Führer Adolf Hitler, who had made no secret of his belief that the Games would demonstrate the superiority of the Aryan people. Hitler could hardly have been proved more wrong: in Berlin Owens and 17 black teammates won 13 of the U.S.'s 23 track and field medals—eight of them gold.

Legend has it that an enraged Hitler snubbed Owens by refusing to shake his hand. That story now appears to have been the concoction of American sportswriters; in fact the opportunity for the two men to shake hands never arose. Nevertheless, Owens himself came to appreciate the moral force of this version of history and included it in his speeches. It did not hurt his legacy that the 1940 and 1944 Games were canceled due to war. The hiatus gave the world a full dozen years in which to savor Owens's grace and the drama of his supposed show-

Owens's heroics on the track in Berlin (opposite page) led to a ticker-tape parade in New York City (above).

Jesse Owens™ Estate of Jesse Owens c/o CMG Worldwide, Indpl, IN..

down with the world's great villain.

The irony in all this, as it turns out, is that Owens had little interest in politics. Soon after returning from Berlin, he sold his services to Republican presidential candidate Alf Landon more for the $15,000 fee Landon was offering than for any strong political conviction.

Landon won just two states. "Poorest race I ever ran," cracked Owens. Later, as the civil rights movement grew stronger, black leaders tried to enlist the great Olympic champion in their cause. Repeatedly, they were rebuffed. Though fleet of foot, Owens always seemed slightly out of step with other African Americans. Indeed, when the forces of the Establishment needed a reliable black hero to "talk sense" to radical members of the 1968 U.S. Olympic team, they

Owens's victory in the 100-meter final (top, left) helped to dash the hopes of Hitler (top, right) for an Aryan-dominated Games; a touching counterpoint to Hitler's racism was the friendship that developed between Owens and German long jumper Luz Long (above); on the way to Berlin aboard the SS *Manhattan*, Owens exhibited a fluid hurdling form, even in street clothes (opposite page).

> **"I let my feet spend as little time on the ground as possible. From the air, fast down, and from the ground, fast up. My foot is only a fraction of time on the track."**
>
> —*JESSE OWENS, 1936*

turned to Owens, who later would publish a book with the curious title *Blackthink: My Life as Black Man and White Man.* In it he stated, "If the Negro doesn't succeed in today's America, it is because he has chosen to fail."

But before judging Owens too harshly, one must remember that Owens was the product of a different era, and his feelings were complicated. He seems to have believed genuinely in the promise of individual advancement afforded by America. Certainly, his own experience confirmed that no-

tion. Owens's grandparents had both been slaves, and his father a sharecropper in tiny Oakville, Alabama. The last of Henry and Mary Owens's 10 surviving children, Jesse had to pick 100 pounds of cotton a day by the time he was seven. When he was nine, his family moved to Cleveland as part of the mass migration of blacks from the rural south to the industrial north. In Cleveland, Owens's sense of racial inequity was tempered considerably by the fact that Charles Riley, his beloved track coach at Fairmount Junior High, was white.

Owens set three world records at the Big Ten meet in 1935 (right), just one of the accomplishments that helped him draw crowds wherever he ran (below); Owens remained close to junior high-school coach Riley (opposite page, center) through high school and after he went to Ohio State.

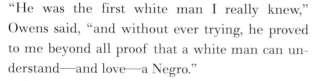

"He was the first white man I really knew," Owens said, "and without ever trying, he proved to me beyond all proof that a white man can understand—and love—a Negro."

Owens attended Ohio State, but was never much of a student and did not graduate. It was as a Buckeye, however, that he achieved the first half of his legend. On May 25, 1935, at the Big Ten championships in Ann Arbor, Michigan, he broke three world records and tied a fourth, all in the space of 45 minutes, running 9.4 for 100 yards (the tie); long

jumping 26' 8¼" (a record that would stand 25 years); clocking 20.3 for 220 yards and 22.6 for the 220 hurdles. Never has anyone set so many world records in such a short period of time.

Owens's athletic career was surprisingly short. By the time he turned 23, in 1936, he had been forced into retirement by the vindictive leaders of the American Olympic Committee, who suspended him for refusing to travel from London to Stockholm to run in the meet following the Olympics. Once home, Owens began to capitalize on his

newfound fame in order to support his wife, Ruth, and their three daughters.

In middle age, Owens became reasonably wealthy by serving as spokesman for a variety of corporations, from Atlantic Richfield Company and Quaker Oats to American Express and Sears. When his 35-year smoking habit finally caught up with him on March 31, 1980, Owens died a symbol not just of athletic greatness but also of the difficult, infinitely complex relationship between black and white Americans in this century.

Aftermath

In the 13 Olympic Games that have been contested since 1936, three athletes have won both the 100 and 200: Americans Bobby Morrow (1956) and Carl Lewis ('84), and Valery Borzov of the Soviet Union ('72). Only Lewis, however, has duplicated Owens's feat of also winning the long jump. In 1984 Lewis won gold medals in the same four events Owens had. He added gold medals in the 100 and long jump in 1988, in the long jump and 4 x 100 relay in '92 and in the long jump in '96. That tied U.S. discus thrower Al Oerter's streak of winning an event in four straight Games.

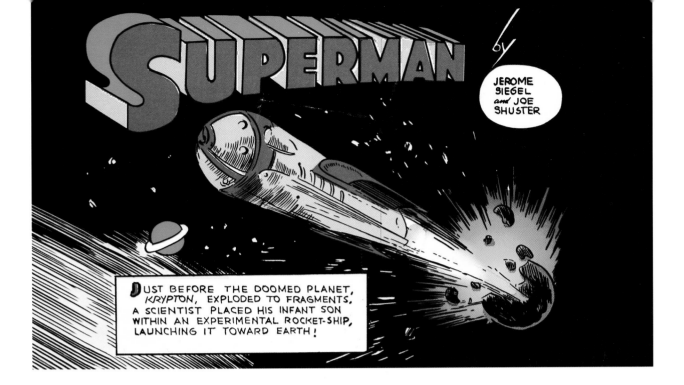

JUST BEFORE THE DOOMED PLANET, *KRYPTON*, EXPLODED TO FRAGMENTS, A SCIENTIST PLACED HIS INFANT SON WITHIN AN EXPERIMENTAL ROCKET-SHIP, LAUNCHING IT TOWARD EARTH!

SUPERMAN

While most people know that Superman came to Earth from the planet Krypton, few are aware that the Man of Steel was actually born in Cleveland.

It's true, the most famous comic book super hero of all, indeed, the one who made it possible for all of the others to exist, came to life in 1933 in the unsung city by the shores of Lake Erie. The brainchild of two teenagers, writer Jerry Siegel and illustrator Joe Shuster, Superman was meant to be, in Siegel's words, "like Samson, Hercules, and all the strongmen I ever heard tell of rolled into one. *Only more so.*"

He was also a bad guy at first, but his creators quickly scrapped that idea and opted for the now-familiar legend of the alien from Krypton who disguises himself as mild-mannered reporter Clark Kent. With his superhuman powers, which include the ability to fly, he devotes his life to fighting crime. Though the hero's look changed over time, a few basic elements were in place at the start, including the red "S" emblazoned on his chest and the flowing red cape trailing behind him. Publishers were unanimous in their response. "Preposterous," they keened on their rejection slips. "Outlandish." "No one would believe it."

Siegel and Shuster received 17 rejections before they shelved the Man of Steel and went to New York City to work for Detective Comics (DC) in 1938. Comic books were still in their infancy at the time, and much of their material was reprinted from daily newspaper strips such as Dick Tracy and Mutt and Jeff. Most comic books were sold as premiums tied to other products, and few publishers saw them as

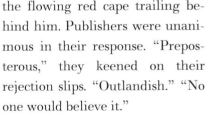

Superman's origins (above) were explained in 1939 in the first comic book devoted exclusively to him (opposite page).

Comic panels (left)

WHEN THE VESSEL REACHED OUR PLANET, THE CHILD WAS FOUND BY AN ELDERLY COUPLE, THE KENTS.

LOOK, MARY! — IT'S A CHILD!

THE POOR THING! — ITS BEEN ABANDONED!

THE INFANT WAS TURNED OVER TO AN ORPHAN ASYLUM, WHERE IT ASTOUNDED THE ATTENDANTS WITH ITS FEATS OF STRENGTH.

WE — WE COULDN'T GET THAT SWEET CHILD OUT OF OUR MIND.

WE'VE COME TO ADOPT HIM IF YOU'LL PERMIT US.

I BELIEVE IT CAN BE ARRANGED. (—WHEW! THANK GOODNESS THEY'RE TAKING HIM AWAY BEFORE HE WRECKS THE ASYLUM!-)

THE LOVE AND GUIDANCE OF HIS KINDLY FOSTER-PARENTS WAS TO BECOME AN IMPORTANT FACTOR IN THE SHAPING OF THE BOY'S FUTURE.

NOW LISTEN TO ME, CLARK! THIS GREAT STRENGTH OF YOURS —YOU'VE GOT TO HIDE IT FROM PEOPLE OR THEY'LL BE SCARED OF YOU!

BUT WHEN THE PROPER TIME COMES, YOU MUST USE IT TO ASSIST HUMANITY,

"**Faster than a speeding bullet. More powerful than a locomotive. Able to leap tall buildings in a single bound.... Look! Up in the sky ... it's a bird!... It's a plane!... It's Superman!**"

—*Radio announcer,*
Adventures of Superman, 1940

independent entities, much less as a medium capable of launching its own star.

Harry Donenfeld's fledgling DC, however, had an inkling of the comic book's potential. DC was always on the lookout for worthy original material. In 1938, while readying the premiere issue of DC's *Action Comics*, editor Vincent Sullivan found a copy of Siegel's and Shuster's wild creation on his desk. The freelance editor Sheldon Mayer had put it there, thinking Superman might be a good fit for *Action Comics*. To Siegel's and Shuster's surprise, Sullivan not only bought Superman, but also decided to put the Man of Steel on the cover of *Action Comics* No. 1 (June 1938).

Donenfeld, for his part, was not so sanguine about the new character's prospects. When he saw the cover of *Action* No. 1, which pictures Superman hoisting a car overhead and smashing the vehicle into a boulder as terror-stricken crooks flee, "he got really worried," Mayer recalled. "He felt that nobody would believe it, that it was

The basic story of the interplanetary tot (left) who grew up to become a "champion of the oppressed" (opposite page),

"sworn to devote his existence to helping those in need," remained a constant throughout the Man of Steel's many iterations.

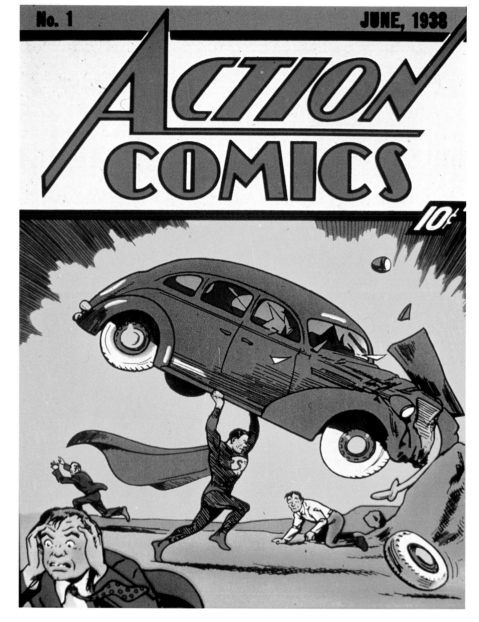

Shuster (top) and Siegel (above) endured rejection after rejection before their superpowered creation landed on the cover of *Action Comics* No. I in June 1938 (right).

ridiculous." But by the end of that summer, children were asking not for *Action Comics* but for "the comic with Superman in it." The following year DC began publishing a quarterly comic devoted exclusively to Superman. As sales climbed, it became apparent that Superman's heroics extended beyond the pages of *Action*: Thanks to his success, the medium of comic books had become a viable form. And then some. A copy of *Action Comics* No. 1 sold for $82,500 in 1992.

That was also the year in which Superman was killed by the notorious villain Doomsday in the most widely read comic in history, *Superman* No. 75. But Superman would be back. Indeed he has been a resilient and versatile hero. When Siegel and Shuster left DC in the mid-'40s, a series of talented writers and illustrators took over the reigns. DC also ushered Superman into Hollywood and onto television. By 1948 Superman had appeared in three comic books, had his own newspaper strip, starred in a radio show (on which the classic introduction, "It's a bird!... It's a plane!... It's Super-

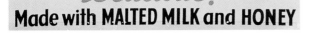

Aftermath

Following the fourth and final film in which Christopher Reeve starred as the Man of Steel, *Superman IV: The Quest for Peace* (1987), the hero's fate took some surprising turns in the pages of DC Comics. In 1991 Clark Kent revealed his true identity to his longtime love interest, Lois Lane. Superman's demise in 1992 was followed by his 1993 revival. In 1997 Superman was completely overhauled. He assumed new powers, becoming an energy-based being, and took on a new look as well. Gone was the trademark red, blue and yellow costume, and in its place was a sleek blue-and-white "containment suit."

In 1998 the changes grew even more extreme: Superman split into two separate heroes, Superman Red and Superman Blue. However, in June 1998, sixty years after the man of steel made his debut in Action Comics, a unified Superman returned, once again clad in his traditional costume.

Another TV series, *Lois and Clark: The New Adventures of Superman,* had a successful four-year run in the '90s and made stars of its two leads, Dean Cain and Teri Hatcher.

Superman's national popularity spawned a variety of products, including a Superman doll (right) and Superman bread (above), both of which debuted in 1942.

man!" was coined) and was the subject of a novel and a 15-episode movie serial. In 1951 the television series, *Adventures of Superman*, debuted. The show, starring George Reeves, was produced until 1957, and has remained on the air in syndication ever since.

By the time Christopher Reeve portrayed him in 1978's *Superman*, the Man of Steel had traveled a long way from Krypton, and Cleveland. He had become an American icon.

THE NEW DEAL

It would be hard to exaggerate the despair that gripped the United States at the start of 1933. "We could smell the depression in the air that historically cruel winter which chilled so many of us like a world's end," wrote Harold Clurman, author of *The Fervent Years*. "It was like a raw wind; the very houses we lived in seemed to be shrinking." More than 15 million Americans had lost their jobs and more than 5,000 banks had collapsed, wiping out nine million savings accounts. In three years the nation's industrial production plummeted from $949 million to just $74 million, driving working people to take desperate measures. In New York City's Central Park a couple lived in a cave, while in Chicago a group of 55 men was arrested for dismantling an entire four-story building and carrying the bricks off to sell. Across America were thousands of thin, dirty children, dressed in

tatters. In a stinging rebuke of the nation's ineffective leader, the vast homeless encampments found in virtually every U.S. city came to be known as "Hoovervilles."

Herbert Hoover, who had made his reputation by managing the recovery of the Mississippi River valley following the great flood of 1927, seemed incapable of coping with this disaster. In the months leading up to the 1932 presidential election it was widely assumed that the Democratic candidate would beat him easily. When the delegates chose Franklin Delano Roosevelt, who as governor of New York from 1929 to 1933 oversaw the most ambitious recovery program in the country, Roosevelt flew to Chicago to accept the nomination personally. There, he made a grand, ringing promise:

"I pledge you, I pledge myself, to a new deal for the American people."

Projects such as the Coulee Dam (left) and programs like the Civilian Conservation Corps (top) got the nation moving again.

Charles R. Macauley, a cartoonist for *The Mirror* zeroed in on the phrase "new deal" and used it the following day, and the name stuck. After winning office in a landslide, Roosevelt launched the greatest expansion of federal power in the nation's history.

Roosevelt thought of himself as a commander in chief waging a desperate war on domestic soil. Nothing could interfere with his plans. He immediately declared a bank holiday, and on March 12, 1933, in the very first of his calming "fireside chats" on national radio, urged, "I can assure you that it is safer to keep your money in a reopened bank than under the mattress. Let us unite in banishing fear."

Thus began the whirlwind of legislative activity that came to be known as the "Hundred Days." In that brief giddy span Roosevelt rammed through Congress 15 major pieces of legislation giving birth to an endless new alphabet of commissions and programs, some of which, like the Securities and Exchange Commission (SEC) and

The artistic legacy of the WPA includes the Hollywood Bowl (above), the City Hall in Kansas City, Missouri (right), and the mural in the California State House created by artist Lucile Lloyd (above, right); through generators like the ones at Wilson Dam (opposite page) in Alabama, the TVA supplied electricity to millions for the first time.

the Tennessee Valley Authority (TVA), survive today. To combat unemployment he persuaded Congress to appropriate $500 million for the Civilian Conservation Corps (CCC), and to guarantee bank deposits he established the Federal Deposit Insurance Corporation (FDIC). Understanding the historical role of the farmer in the U.S. economy, Roosevelt created the Agricultural Adjustment Administration (AAA) to regulate farm prices.

The centerpiece of Roosevelt's early efforts was the National Industrial Recovery Act (NIRA), which established a minimum wage and a maximum number of work-hours, and created both the National Recovery Administration (NRA) and the Public Works Administration (PWA) to undertake large construction projects. Some two million employers signed the NRA agreement, which entitled them to display proudly the Blue Eagle thunder-

"We have always known that heedless self-interest was bad morals; we know now that it is bad economics."
—FRANKLIN DELANO ROOSEVELT, inaugural address, January 20, 1937

A YOUNG MAN'S OPPORTUNITY

CCC

FOR WORK PLAY STUDY & HEALTH

APPLICATIONS TAKEN BY
ILLINOIS EMERGENCY RELIEF COMMISSION
ILLINOIS SELECTING AGENCY

Rolling logs in California State Redwood Park (opposite page, above), planting trees as part of the CCC's ambitious reforestation project (opposite page, inset), cleaning up after a flood in Louis- **ville (above)—everywhere you looked, New Deal programs were putting people to work.**

bird emblem bearing the words "We Do Our Part" in their windows.

The PWA metamorphosed into the Works Progress Administration (WPA), which, from 1935 to 1943, employed a total of 8.5 million people on 1.4 million separate projects, including the construction of 8,000 parks, 800 airports, 3,300 storage dams, 78,000 bridges and 650,000 miles of roads. One almost wonders whether the United States was virgin landscape before Roo-

sevelt's volunteer army began its many labors.

The New Deal momentum slowed a bit when, on May 27, 1935, Charles Evans Hughes, the chief justice of the United States Supreme Court, read the Court's unanimous decision in the Schechter poultry case, in which four brothers from Brooklyn were accused of violating provisions of the NRA by, among other actions, selling diseased chickens and disregarding wage and hour stipulations. "This is the end of the centralization," warned Hughes, "and I want you to go back and tell the president that we're not going to let this government centralize everything." Annoyed but hardly cowed, Roosevelt launched

what became known as the Second New Deal. It included the Social Security Act of 1935, which established a system of welfare payments and provided insurance for the elderly, the disabled and the sick.

Roosevelt's programs could not end the Depression all by themselves; ultimately, nothing less than the industrial boost brought on by World War II would restore the nation to full prosperity. Still, Roosevelt's intelligence and can-do spirit were invaluable in restoring the morale of the American people.

Aftermath

America's next sweeping social and economic program was the Great Society, which Lyndon Baines Johnson introduced in May 1964, while campaigning for the presidency against Republican candidate Barry Goldwater. "The Great Society rests on abundance and liberty for all," said Johnson. "It demands an end to poverty and racial injustice, to which we are totally committed in our time."

Among the legislation and programs that comprised Johnson's Great Society were the Civil Rights Bill of 1964 and the Voting Rights Act of 1965, in addition to Project Head Start, the Job Corps, Medicaid and Medicare. Debate continues over the effectiveness of many Great Society programs.

LIFE

NOVEMBER 23, 1936 **10** CENTS

LIFE MAGAZINE

To see life; to see the world; to eyewitness great events; to watch the faces of the poor and gestures of the proud; to see strange things—machines, armies, multitudes, shadows in the jungle and on the moon; to see man's work—his paintings, towers and discoveries; to see things thousands of miles away, things hidden behind walls and within rooms, things dangerous to come to; the women that men love and many children; to see and to take pleasure in seeing; to see and be amazed; to see and be instructed....

Such was the broad, timeless mission that founding editor Henry Luce articulated for *Life* magazine as its November 1936 debut approached. Luce, just 36 years old, was already a veteran publisher: Three years after graduating from Yale he had cofounded *Time* magazine, fol-

lowed by *Fortune* seven years later. Of the three periodicals, though, *Life* would best reflect his eclectic hunger for knowledge and experience of things large and small, topical and arcane.

The way Luce saw it, "The photograph is an extraordinary instrument for correcting that really inherent evil in journalism, which is its unbalance between the good news and the bad." But the actual idea of a picture magazine—capitalizing on the advent of the highly portable 35mm camera—came from Luce's new wife, Clare Boothe Luce, who had previously pitched it, name and all, to an unreceptive Condé Nast. Having the chutzpah to launch a weekly in the midst of the Depression, however, was pure Henry. Equally bold was his decision to give the magazine an oversize

The idea for *Life*, whose first issue (opposite page) appeared in 1936, was not Henry's (above, left), but Clare's (above, right).

LIFE Magazine ©1936 Time Inc.

format, using expensive "coated" paper to better showcase the photographs. Spread open, a copy of *Life* would measure a gargantuan 13½ by 21 inches.

Beginning with the premiere issue, *Life* towered—literally and figuratively—over virtually all the other magazines in the rack. For the first cover, Luce selected a dramatic, nearly abstract photograph by prominent industrial photographer Margaret Bourke-White. In it the starkly geometric walls of Montana's Fort Peck Dam dwarf two human figures. The dual impact of the photograph and the magazine's large format was stunning.

The accompanying story marked the birth of the photographic essay in the United States. Nine pages of Bourke-White's photos poignantly captured the lives of 10,000 relief workers and their families living in shantytowns near the dam, a Works Progress Administration (WPA) project. In one photo caption, Archibald MacLeish, who would later gain fame as a poet and playwright, wrote, "A relief project started the new Wild West," where settlements were "short on sanitation, long on bars."

When the magazine hit the newsstands on

In *Life*'s first photo essay, Bourke-White (below), showed her range by depicting life on an intimate scale in photographs of Fort Peck nightlife (opposite page) and on a grander one in shots of the pipes (right) used to divert a section of the Missouri River during the construction of the Fort Peck Dam.

"The first issue of a magazine is not the magazine. It is the beginning."

—LIFE'S *EDITORS, introducing their November 23, 1936, edition*

Thursday, November 19, it caused a minor riot. All 466,000 issues disappeared within four hours. Vendors barraged Time Inc.'s New York offices with telephone and telegraph pleas for more copies; the presses churned out page after page until there was no paper left. Readers lucky enough to have obtained an issue were treated to 96 pages of stories and departments ranging from "*Life* on the American Newsfront"—a photo and caption montage of quirky, comical and sobering stories from around the country—to "Black Widow," a series of 22 photographs with captions devoted to the enemies, mating habits, and parenting practices of the unsentimental arachnid.

The issue opened with a daringly graphic full-page shot of an obstetrician holding a newborn baby by the ankles. The photo bore the playful title "*Life* Begins." The issue closed with a photo essay on French blue bloods hunting partridges, hares and pheasants in the first installment of an ongoing feature entitled "*Life* Goes to a Party." That section became so popular that readers soon took to leafing through the magazine from back to front.

But *Life*'s unexpected instant success came at

BOYS WITH WINGS

JANUARY 30, 1939 **10** CENTS

STUDENT NURSES

JANUARY 31, 1938 **10** CENTS

WORLD'S FAIR: "AMERICAN BEAUTIES"

MARCH 13, 1939 **10** CENTS

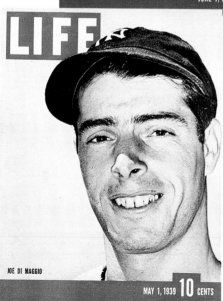

JUNE 7, 1937 **10** CENTS

JULY CORN

JULY 5, 1937 **10** CENTS

Classic *Life* **images from covers published in 1936 through 1939, simple in approach but powerful in emotional impact, included (top row, left to right): an air cadet, student nurses and a World's Fair sculpture; (middle row, left to right): saddle shoes and July corn; (bottom row, left to right): Yankee star Joe DiMaggio, a Czech soldier and the Metropolitan Opera Ballet.**

JOE DI MAGGIO

MAY 1, 1939 **10** CENTS

ARMS AND THE MEN

OCTOBER 3, 1938 **10** CENTS

METROPOLITAN OPERA'S BALLET

DECEMBER 28, 1936 **10** CENTS

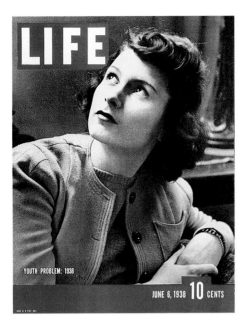

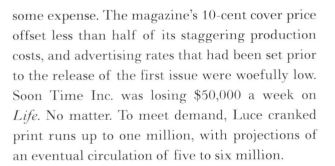

More classic '30s covers (clockwise from above): a couple at a marriage clinic, a parachute test, an issue devoted to the "youth problem" and garment workers at play.

Aftermath

From a start-up staff of 19 people in three offices (New York, Paris and London), *Life* grew to have 251 staffers in 28 bureaus and 317 part-time correspondents, or stringers, by 1956. At its peak in 1969, *Life* was read by one in every four American citizens and wielded tremendous influence over how the country saw itself. The emotional response it evoked through its photography, especially in times of war, had an extraordinary and lasting impact on news media of all sorts.

In 1978 *Life* became a monthly and though its circulation today is not as large as it was at its peak as a weekly, the magazine continues to uphold the tradition of journalistic excellence for which it is justly famous.

Henry Luce, perhaps the greatest innovator in print journalism, died in 1967 at the age of 68.

some expense. The magazine's 10-cent cover price offset less than half of its staggering production costs, and advertising rates that had been set prior to the release of the first issue were woefully low. Soon Time Inc. was losing $50,000 a week on *Life*. No matter. To meet demand, Luce cranked print runs up to one million, with projections of an eventual circulation of five to six million.

By bringing the world home to Americans in a glorious alliance of spectacle and intimacy, Luce had placed his finger squarely on the country's pulse. *Life* became one of the most widely read magazines in American history.

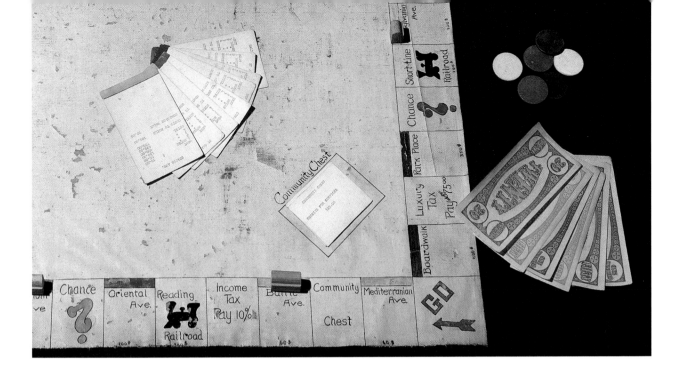

MONOPOLY

In the midst of the Depression, a homemade board game turned thousands of impoverished Americans into fantasy real-estate barons and made Charles Darrow, an unemployed heating engineer, a millionaire.

Like 25 percent of the American work force, Darrow, a family man from Germantown, Pennsylvania, found himself jobless after the stock market crash of 1929. He spent the early '30s seeking employment, repairing electric irons and walking dogs for anyone willing to pay him. For the most part, though, he had  a lot of spare time to tinker and reflect on more prosperous days. Then he hit pay dirt. Sitting at his kitchen table one evening in 1933, Darrow began drawing a circular game board on his tablecloth. After filling its spaces with the names of streets that abutted Atlantic City's boardwalk, he added the names of the three railroads and the utility companies that served the town, appending a fourth railroad, the Short Line, to keep the board symmetrical. He crafted houses and hotels from scraps of wood, and Chance, Community Chest and title cards for the properties from cardboard. With a pair of dice, a stack of play money and colored buttons for markers, the game was ready to play.

The allure of feeling rich and powerful was especially strong during the Depression, and Darrow's game was an instant hit with his neighbors. Every evening they joined the Darrows in a rousing round of real-estate development that allowed them to manipulate fantastic sums of money from a bank that never ran out. The night's winner of-

Darrow (opposite page) worked tirelessly to popularize his early version of the MONOPOLY game (above).

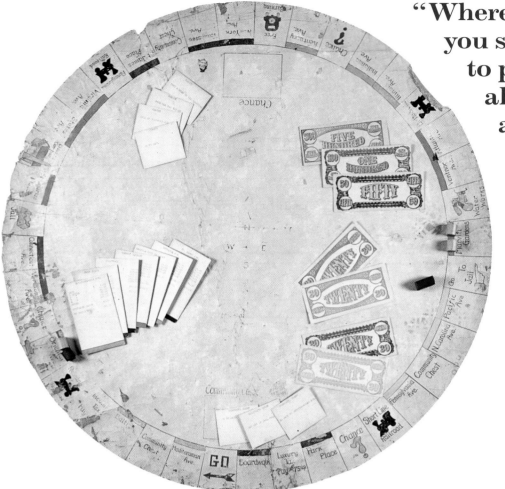

ten asked for a MONOPOLY set of his or her own, and before long Darrow was making one a day and selling them for four dollars apiece.

Encouraged by the success of his handmade version, Darrow sent the game to Parker Brothers, but the 50-year-old company, which was itself feeling the sting of the Depression, was wary. Parker Brothers had a longstanding set of inviolable ground rules for "family games," and, according to a company executive, the MONOPOLY game violated them in 52 ways. A family game should last about 45 minutes: Playing the MONOPOLY game could take hours. A game should have a specific goal, such as reaching the jackpot at the end of the board: In the MONOPOLY game players circled the board endlessly with the nebulous aim of staying solvent and bankrupting opponents. A game's rules should be simple: MONOPOLY players would be confused by having to manage mortgages, rents and interest. Like a round of the MONOPOLY game, the list of infractions went on and on.

Perturbed but not discouraged, Darrow enlisted a printer friend to help him mass-produce the game. Philadelphia department stores such as Wanamaker's placed enormous orders for the game, which was developing an avid local following. But it wasn't until the game went as far as

Darrow's MONOPOLY (opposite page) was enhanced by the character of Rich Uncle Pennybags (right and above), which was added by Parker Brothers after it bought the game from Darrow in 1935.

Boston and FAO Schwarz in New York that word got back to Parker Brothers. In early 1935 Robert Barton, the president of Parker Brothers, offered to buy the game from Darrow and give him royalties on each set sold. Darrow took the money and ran—to Bucks County, Pennsylvania, where at age 46 he became a gentleman farmer, world traveler and collector of exotic orchid species. Asked why he had sold out to Parker Brothers, Darrow stated, "Taking the precepts of MONOPOLY to heart, I did not care to speculate."

Parker Brothers modified the MONOPOLY game's board and some of its cards and added metal objects such as the car and top hat as tokens. Although Parker Brothers was turning out 20,000 MONOPOLY games a week by February 1935, the cautious company considered the game an adult fad, so just prior to the 1936 Christmas season founder George Parker stopped production on the game "against the possibility of a very early slump." Wrong again. MONOPOLY enjoyed enormous sales that season and went on to become the most popular twentieth-century board game in the world.

Aftermath

As of 1998, the MONOPOLY game was being published in 80 countries and 26 languages. The U.S. Spanish language edition is sold in 12 countries. Parker Brothers, now owned by Hasbro, has sold more than 200 million sets. Among MONOPOLY's many versions have been a 1930s Deluxe edition, which included large, gold-toned tokens; a 1964 steel-backed, 95-pound laminated set for New England Divers; a 1978 Neiman Marcus full-size chocolate game; a 1991 Franklin Mint edition that included gold and silver pieces; and a World Cup France 98 edition for soccer enthusiasts. But the real beauty of the MONOPOLY game is that the cost of living in the game has never increased. If it had, the rent on Boardwalk would have gone from its original $50 to $610.28 in 1995 and the rent for one house on Park Place would have risen from $175 to $2,135.99.

ELEANOR ROOSEVELT

There was no reason for anyone who met her to suspect that young Eleanor Roosevelt was destined for greatness, that she would utterly transform the role of First Lady and become perhaps the most beloved and important American woman of the twentieth century. The woman who would win the world's affection and respect by comforting the sick and speaking for the needy had herself been a frightened, unhappy child. "I was not only timid," Eleanor recalled, "I was afraid. Afraid of almost everything, I think: of mice, of the dark, of imaginary dangers."

Born on October 11, 1884, to upper-crust socialite New Yorkers Elliott and Anna Hall Roosevelt, Eleanor was so solemn and humorless that her mother nicknamed her Granny. Tall and unprepossessing, with buck teeth, she was painfully conscious of the contrast she made with her stylish mother. "My mother was troubled by my lack of beauty," she wrote in her autobiography. "I knew it as a child senses these things. She tried hard to bring me up well so that my manners would compensate for my looks, but her efforts only made me more keenly conscious of my shortcomings."

Self-conscious around her mother, Eleanor adored her father, whose older brother Teddy had cut such a dashing figure as president at the turn of the century. But this too brought grief as Elliott was a pathetic bundle of nerves, an alcoholic and a drug user. At age seven, after the death of her mother, Eleanor went to live with her maternal grandmother in a gloomy Manhattan brownstone; her father died two years later. Life was miserable under her grandmother's stern eye, but it improved markedly when, at age 14, she was sent overseas to Allenswood, a small finishing school on the outskirts of London. Eleanor, who felt freed from her family prison, later described her days there as the happiest of her life.

That same year Eleanor met her distant cousin,

In her extensive travels, Eleanor (left, and above, right) was the eyes and ears for her husband the president (above, left).

Franklin, at a formal dance. Prodded by a relative, he asked her to dance, which even then Eleanor recognized as a gesture of kindness. But when the two were thrown together a few summers later at the family vacation compound at Campobello, a small island off the coast of Maine, they got on wonderfully. Franklin, 23, and Eleanor, 20, were married on St. Patrick's Day, 1905. Eleanor was given away by her uncle Teddy. Eleanor was not a public person by nature. For a time she was content to lead the life of a political wife. But as her husband climbed from post to post, she watched and learned. She joined the League of Women Voters in 1921, one year after women achieved voting rights. When Franklin developed polio later that year, she was encouraged by Democratic party officials to assume a more active role to keep her husband's name before the public. Having found that she enjoyed the expanded role, in 1924 she addressed the newly formed women's wing at the Democratic convention.

Her awakening political consciousness notwithstanding, Eleanor did not want to become First Lady. "From the personal standpoint, I did not want my husband to be president," she admitted in retrospect. "It was pure selfishness on my part, and I never mentioned my feelings on the subject to him."

It is hard now to imagine FDR's presidency without her. As much as he "invented" the modern presidency, Eleanor totally redefined the unofficial post of First Lady.

"You gain strength, courage and confidence by every experience in which you really stop to look fear in the face. You must do the thing you think you cannot do."

— *ELEANOR ROOSEVELT*

Deeply insecure as a young woman (opposite page, top left), Eleanor found a leavening influence in her marriage to Franklin (opposite page, below) and soon warmed to the roles of public figure (opposite page, top right, with Queen Elizabeth) and mother (above, bottom left, with Franklin [in white hat] and sons James [bottom right], Franklin Jr. and John [middle row, center and right, respectively]).

She was the first wife of a president to hold a press conference, the first to ride in an airplane and the first to drive her own car; she even carried a gun—at the Secret Service's behest—when she drove alone. The hallmark of Roosevelt's presidency was his concern for the lives of ordinary people. One of his key lines of communication with them was Eleanor, who radiated common sense and uncommon compassion. When the Daughters of the American Revolution barred celebrated black singer Marian Anderson from performing in its Washington, D.C., auditorium, Constitution Hall,

Eleanor resigned from the organization, focusing worldwide attention on the issue of racial justice.

Because traveling was something of an ordeal for her disabled husband, she became his eyes and ears, visiting slums in Puerto Rico, coal mines in Ohio and American soldiers around the world. Her nickname was Eleanor Everywhere. As someone once cracked, "Hoover sent the army. Roosevelt sent his wife."

Upon Franklin's death in 1945, Eleanor split her time between a New York City apartment and her home in Val-Kill, a few miles from the Roosevelt family seat in Hyde Park, New York. She continued to travel the world, first as an official delegate to the United Nations under Harry Truman and later as the chair of the United Nations Human Rights Commission. Everywhere she went she was greeted with an outpouring of love and respect. "I have come to learn," she told Prime Minister Jawaharlal Nehru as she climbed out of the plane in India. In 1957, at the age of 73, she traveled to the Soviet Union as a correspondent for the *New York Post* and visited Soviet Premier Nikita S.

Khrushchev at his dacha on the Black Sea. Counseled to take it easy, she said, "I am willing to slow down but I just don't know how."

When Eleanor died of a stroke on November 7, 1962, the world mourned, moved by the life of one who overcame such deep insecurities to give so much to others. "About the only value the story of my life may have," she once wrote, "is to show that one can, even without particular gifts, overcome obstacles that seem insurmountable if one is willing to face the fact that they must be overcome; that, in spite of timidity and fear, in spite of a lack of special talents, one can find a way to live widely and fully."

Indeed, she found many.

Eleanor Everywhere's stops included a coal mine in Ohio (opposite page, top left), a women's farm cooperative in Washington, D.C. (opposite page, top right), Cumberland Homesteads in Tennessee (top) and the United Nations (above); her support for singer Marian Anderson (opposite page, inset) helped focus world attention on issues of racial justice.

Aftermath

Eleanor Roosevelt completely transformed the duties of First Lady, shifting them from the purely ceremonial to the actively altruistic and setting a precedent for many of the women who followed her into the White House.

Subsequent First Ladies have embraced a variety of causes. Nancy Reagan fought drug abuse with the battle cry "Just Say No," and Barbara Bush launched a campaign for literacy. Current First Lady Hillary Rodham Clinton has crusaded around the world for children's rights. Her book on the subject of the community's role in raising healthy children, *It Takes a Village,* was a bestseller in 1996.

BOBBY JONES

On September 27, 1930, at the Merion Cricket Club in Ardmore, Pennsylvania, Bobby Jones defeated Eugene Homans in the final of the U.S. Amateur to complete what stands as a singular achievement in golf: the Grand Slam. No one before Jones had won all four major tournaments—at that time the British Open and Amateur championships and the U.S. Open and Amateur championships—in the same year, and no one has done so since.

Indeed, Jones's golf accomplishments remain unparalleled. Although he competed relatively infrequently and rarely practiced, he won with a consistency that no golfer will ever match. From his first effort—as a 13-year-old—in a senior tournament, the 1915 Southern Amateur, through his triumph at the 1930 U.S. Amateur, he entered only 52 tourna-

ments and won 23. Again and again he beat the game's best players, both professional and amateur. Of the 11 U.S. Opens he entered, Jones won four and was a runner-up in four. He won three of his four British Opens. With the addition of six victories in the U.S. and British Amateurs, he won a total of 13 major championships. Each year from 1923 to '30 he won at least one of the two U.S. national championships. Moreover, he achieved these feats while studying at Georgia Tech, Emory and Harvard, practicing law, and raising a family.

Born in Atlanta on March 17, 1902, Robert T. Jones Jr. was a frail child whose athletic genius developed naturally. After his family moved to a house just off the 13th green of the Atlanta Athletic Club in the suburb of East Lake, the six-year-

Jones (left at the 1930 British Open and above in the first Masters in 1934) was the epitome of the gentleman amateur.

The image of Bobby Jones is officially licensed by the heirs of Robert T. ("Bobby") Jones, Jr.

old Jones learned to play by following the club's Scottish golf professional, Stewart Maiden, around the course and then going off on his own to imitate Maiden's swing. Soon Jones developed a graceful, economic swing of his own.

Though his body took naturally to golf, Jones struggled with the game's demands on his mind. On the one hand he battled the complacency that could fog his focus when he had what seemed to be an insurmountable lead; on the other he strove to quiet a thunderous temper. In the third round of the 1921 British Open, at the par-3 11th hole of the Old Course at St. Andrews, the 19-year-old Jones took five strokes to reach the green. Having shot 46 on the front nine and made a double bogey on the 10th hole, he tore up his scorecard and left the course. Later that summer, in the second round of the 1921 U.S. Amateur, he threw his club after taking a bad shot and it bounced up and struck a woman in the leg. These explosions shocked Jones as much as anyone else, and from then on he held himself to a code of good sportsmanship. With his temper in check, Jones started winning majors, beginning with the 1923 U.S. Open. When he won both the U.S. and the British Opens three years later, he decided that he had it in him to take all four majors in one year. He set his eye on 1930 for the attempt.

On November 18, 1930, only 28 and barely two months after achieving his goal, Jones announced his retirement from competitive golf. Neither the fame nor the pressures that came with his success on the course agreed with his introverted and high-strung nature, and retirement freed him to rediscover the pure joy of the game and to make other contributions to the sport. Some months later, with financier Clifford Roberts and course architect Alister MacKenzie, he cofounded and codesigned the Augusta National Golf Club.

Completed in 1932, Augusta National was built on land that previously nurtured the azalea

"**From this man we learn not only how we may improve our golf games and act like gentlemen, but also how to cope with life, however good or bad it may be.**"

—*BEN CRENSHAW, professional golfer, 1993*

After a couple of test shots in 1932 (opposite page, above), Jones pronounced himself pleased with the progress of construction on Augusta National; two years later, he competed in the first Masters on the course (opposite page, below); the ever-popular Jones appeared in some of golf's earliest instructional films (above).

bushes of Prosper Berckmans, the horticulturist who popularized the azalea in the United States. Its blooming in March and April marks the Augusta National's finest season, during which Jones and Roberts hoped to host the U.S. Open periodically. Because the U.S. Golf Association did not wish to break tradition and hold the event at any time other than June or July, the members of Augusta National decided to inaugurate their own tournament.

The First Annual Invitation Tournament at Augusta was held March 22–25, 1934. The field included current and former U.S. and British champions, several of Jones's friends and Jones himself, who, prior to the competition, briefly flirted with the idea of making a comeback. Instead he took on the role of tournament host. In 1938 the event was officially renamed the Masters. "I must admit it was born of a touch of immodesty," Jones said after consenting to the members' wish to adopt this name for his creation. Only Jones would question his claim on the title.

Jones's many wins included the 1926 U.S. Open (opposite page, below), the 1928 U.S. Amateur (opposite page, above), the 1927 British Open (above left) and the 1930 British Amateur (left); in July 1930, with his Grand Slam half finished, Jones enjoyed a hero's welcome in New York (above).

Aftermath

In 1948 Jones was diagnosed with syringomyelia, a rare disease of the spinal cord. He spent the last years of his life in a wheelchair, but continued gracefully to host the Masters until 1968. Jones died in 1971 and is remembered as much for his dignity in illness as for his excellence on the golf course. Only Ben Hogan came close to achieving another Grand Slam, with his triumphs at three of the four professional majors in 1953. Hogan's near Slam began with a win at the Masters, which, with the rise of the professional game, quickly became one of golf's four professional majors.

STREAMLINE DESIGN

It was the spring of 1934. Bands played and children were let out of school for the day. People lined up by the thousands in cities such as Chicago and Philadelphia. Crowds gathered at rural railroad crossings. Like two diesel-powered messiahs, the Burlington Zephyr and Union Pacific's M–10,000 were plying the country's railroad tracks, ready to transport believers out of the Depression. Though far from fully articulated, the trains' modern, streamline design carried with it the promise of better times to come.

Three years before the Zephyr and M–10,000 toured the country, streamlining was little more than an obscure engineering conceit derived from aerodynamic principles that had been explored since the turn of the century. Then, in 1932, industrial designer Norman Bel Geddes presented *Horizons,* a book filled with renderings of teardrop-shaped cars, torpedo-shaped ocean liners and streamlined trains. As historian Jeffrey Meikle wrote, "By popularizing streamlining when only a few engineers were considering its functional use, [Geddes] made possible the design style of the '30s."

Indeed, Geddes's visions of futuristic trains inspired railroad moguls—who were desperate to recapture ridership lost to automobiles, buses, airplanes and the Depression—to embrace streamlining. It also prompted the Chrysler Corporation to begin developing a streamlined automobile, the Airflow, that hit the market in 1934. Despite a record number of orders, sales of the Airflow were low due to production delays and mechanical defects. While the car never really took off, it did popularize such elements as the enclosed spare tire, simplified horizontal contours and integrated headlights and fenders.

Seduced by the new modernism's sensuous curves and comforted by its simplicity, consumers with disposable income developed an insatiable

Two early streamlined products were 20th Century's J-3a locomotive (opposite page) and General Motors's buses (above).

The streamlined look, evident in the Baltimore and Ohio Railroad's "Royal Blue" (left) and the Pennsylvania Railroad's S-1 Class locomotive (above), was paralleled in airplane designs, like that of the Beechcraft propeller plane (opposite page).

appetite for things streamlined. In addition to Geddes, industrial designers Walter Dorwin Teague, Henry Dreyfuss and Raymond Loewy accommodated the national hunger by applying the principles of streamlining to static objects. While aerodynamics had no legitimate raison d'être in stationary products, the designers, who were in search of a new paradigm, believed that streamlining could minimize friction between user and object. To this end, mechanisms and

electrical elements on everything from toasters to Dictaphones were concealed behind rounded forms of plastic and metal alloys—inexpensive materials perfectly suited to mass production.

Although the Art Deco movement of the 1920s and streamline design are often confused, industrial designers of the '30s in the main viewed Art Deco as the superficial application of decorative details to objects and spaces. Where the angular, zigzagging lines of Art Deco echoed the exuberant

80

"The world of the 1930s was especially fond of a particular line, a curved line...a line with a sharp parabolic curve at the end, which it called 'the streamline.'"

—*MARTIN GREIF, author of* Depression Modern, *1975*

beat of assembly-line production, streamline design's simple, spare lines acted as a visual salve in a time of social and economic chaos. In its unifying simplicity, streamlining was an apt metaphor for a country pared down to the basic elements.

While it is difficult to determine the precise role that design, as opposed to advertising and pricing, plays in influencing consumer spending, Loewy's radical modernization of the Sears Coldspot refrigerator in 1935 was an undeniable factor when sales for the model shot up 400 percent, making Sears the market leader. By commissioning slight modifications in the years to come, Sears would enjoy the benefits of planned obsolescence, the kind of marketing-driven restyling that had given birth to industrial design as a profession a decade earlier. But if "modern" product design had been a boon to manufacturers in the '20s, it became an economic necessity in the '30s in that it offered the best

hope for reversing the trend of underconsumption that was stifling the country's economy.

Having streamlined every conceivable vehicle, gadget and gizmo, packaging included, designers began broadening their scope of influence. In 1938, Dreyfuss was commissioned to redesign the 20th Century Limited locomotive and passenger cars, for which he dictated every detail down to the matchbooks and porters' uniforms. Teague, whose renderings of streamlined storefronts for the Pittsburgh Plate Glass Co. were being recreated on main streets across America, came to see the industrial designer's sphere as the entire man-made environment, as did fellow designer Geddes. Their vision of a harmonious machine-age world culminated in pavilion and exhibit designs at the New York World's Fair of 1939.

But if many people were intrigued by the notion

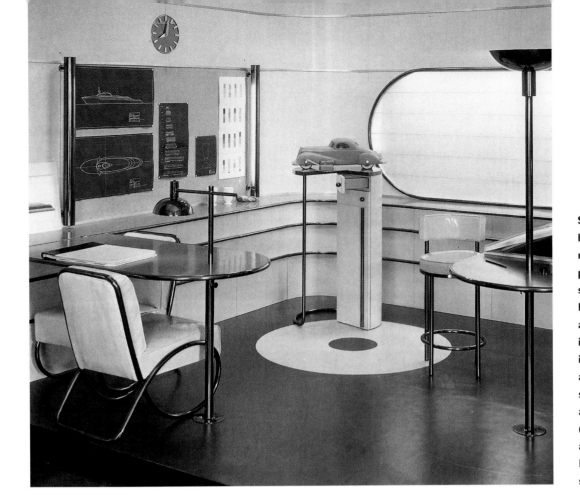

Streamline design, which had a legitimate aerodynamic function in trains, planes and automobiles such as the Airstream De Soto (below), played a purely decorative role in numerous products including clocks, toasters and telephones (opposite page below), as well as in office interiors (left) and club cars such as the one conceived by Henry Dreyfuss (opposite page, top).

of a frictionless planned environment, most bristled at the denial of individual expression inherent in Teague's and Geddes's messianic vision of streamline design. While industrial design's quest to enhance man's interaction with machine-age products culminated in America's first authentic design vernacular, it fell short of transporting the country from the Depression into a new paradigm for modern living.

Aftermath

When World War II ended, Americans had lost their taste for streamlining, whose impersonal, overarching design vision was disturbingly reminiscent of German and Russian totalitarianism. In their eagerness to compensate for 15 years of material deprivation they returned to the rabid consumerism of the 1920s. But most designers had taken in-house jobs with big corporations, where, with little room for idealism, they labored for maximum profit. Vintage streamlined products are now collectors' items and the style is enjoying a resurgence as appliance makers such as Sunbeam and Waring reissue streamline designs.

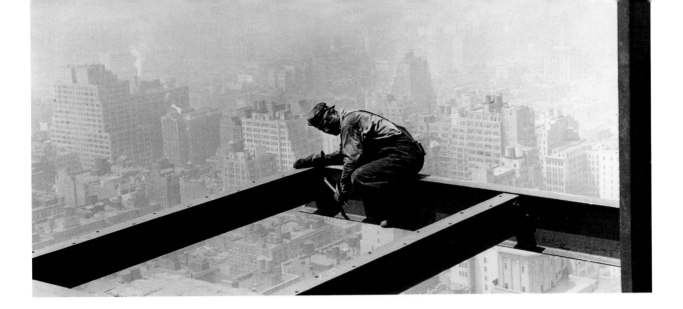

THE EMPIRE STATE BUILDING

Scratch the venerable limestone surface of the Empire State Building and you'll uncover the story of America's passage from the can-do optimism of the 1920s to the hopelessness of the Depression. The plot pits human effort and long-range vision against market forces and myopia.

Thanks to advances in elevator technology and the use of steel in construction, skyscraper fever gripped the nation in the mid-'20s. On drawing boards from Detroit to Philadelphia architects hatched plans for structures that would top the Eiffel Tower in Paris or New York City's Woolworth Building, edifices that would rank, if only briefly, as the world's tallest building. Many schemes never materialized, but enough did that by 1929 the United States counted 377 buildings of 20 stories or more.

Real-estate experts were telling cautionary tales of increasing vacancy rates as early as 1926. But for every pessimist there was an optimist

with cash to burn and another with visions of grandeur. Neither wealthy former General Motors executive John J. Raskob nor four-time governor of New York and 1928 Democratic presidential nominee Al Smith had experience in real estate, but both were excited about Manhattan's lot number 41 on block number 835. The site, occupied by the once preeminent Waldorf-Astoria Hotel at the intersection of Fifth Avenue and 34th Street, would become home to the Empire State Building, a modernist skyscraper offering maximum natural light, high-speed elevators and the finest, most complete service available.

On the late September day in 1929 when wrecking crews began knocking down the old hotel's Victorian walls, commercial buildings in the nation's 23 largest cities were suffering vacancy rates of almost 12 percent. Yet the construction boom continued. Just 10 blocks away from lot 41, the steel

Workers (above) on the Empire State Building (opposite page) ventured "almost as high as the sky," according to Smith.

Through Lamb's engineering know-how and the intrepid spirit of the men who worked on the project (below), it took only 18 months to travel from the building's early stages (left) to the gala dedication attended by Smith and his grandchildren (opposite page) on May 1, 1931.

"In that giant shaft I see a groping toward beauty and spiritual vision. I am one of those who see and yet believe."

—*HELEN KELLER,*
after a trip to the
observation deck in 1933

height of 1,048 feet. Raskob and Smith in turn added six floors to beat Chrysler by two feet and, for good measure, topped the 86th floor with a 200-foot-tall dirigible mooring mast for a total of 102 stories, or 1,250 feet. The mast proved to be a costly, if aesthetically successful, boondoggle, but because of it the Empire State Building would reign as the world's tallest building for 40 years, until 1972, when New York's World Trade Center supplanted it.

The real achievement, though, was not the height of the building so much as the remarkable precision and speed with which it rose. The distribution of materials—including 60,000 tons of steel framing, 10 million bricks, 100,000 rivets, 6,500 windows and 50 miles of pipe—and the movements of up to 3,000 workers representing 60 trades were expertly orchestrated with the help of an ingenious system of chutes, hoppers, elevators and hand-powered rail cars. Steelworkers, who in the words of Smith moved about "almost as high as the sky with as little fear apparently as we walk the streets," erected the frame at the record-breaking pace of 4½ floors per week. So tight was the schedule that, according to architect Richmond Shreve, "There were days when the messenger reached Pittsburgh with drawings

frame of the Chrysler Building was rising fast in its race to surpass the 71-story Bank of Manhattan Building, under construction at 40 Wall Street, as the nation's tallest structure.

Raskob, who had an old score to settle with Chrysler, instructed his architects at the firm of Shreve, Lamb & Harmon to go higher still. Chrysler countered by adding a spire, for a total

Two of the few exceptions to the Empire State Building's restrained design are the building's entrance (right) and its ornate lobby (above); during its early years, the building dwarfed its neighbors (above right), a fact best appreciated from the 86th-floor observation deck (opposite page).

only an hour before the steel mills started rolling the I-beams we would need a few days later."

Between the initial sketch phase and the ribbon cutting ceremony on May 1, 1931, a mere 18 months had passed. And the building came in $8 million under the $50 million budget. Although the design had been fast-tracked to meet the ambitious deadline (as the steel rose for the 30th floor, design details for lower floors were still being worked out), William Lamb received the Architectural League's Medal of Honor in 1931. Working in the new modernist style, Lamb had put function and technology first and kept the design elements stunningly simple, especially compared with those of the exuberantly decorative Chrysler Building.

More than 5,000 visitors viewed New York from the Empire State Building's 86th-floor observation deck on opening day; a total of 775,000 made the climb in the first year. Publicists had a field day measuring everything from ocean liners to pancakes against the new colossus. But no

amount of publicity or professional recognition could keep the Empire State Building from being dubbed the Empty State Building: Six months after it opened, it was less than 25 percent occupied. And the thousands of workers who had erected it were now unemployed and passing from relief lines to bread lines.

The cinematic exploits of King Kong and Fay Ray in 1933 may have prompted a surge of visitors to the skyscraper's observation decks, but in 1936, the building was still empty from the 41st floor up, with the exception of NBC's 85th-floor offices, and there was no happy ending in sight. "The facade that launched a thousand souvenirs," as the modernist icon has been described, would teeter on the verge of bankruptcy until the New Deal and World War II put the nation back to work.

Aftermath

Having barely survived the Depression, the Empire State Building began turning a profit in 1950. It sustained another hard blow, but no structural damage, on July 28, 1945, when a B-25 bomber crashed into the 78th and 79th floors. In May 1976, the 50 millionth visitor rode to the building's 86th-floor observation deck, which attracts more than two million visitors annually. The Empire State Building has appeared in more than 100 movies, from *An Affair to Remember* (1957) to *Sleepless in Seattle* (1993). Next to the Eiffel Tower in Paris, it is the most famous urban icon in the world. In 1972 the first of the World Trade Center towers replaced the Empire State Building as the tallest building in the world. Since 1997, the Petronas Twin Towers of Kuala Lumpur, Malaysia, have held the title.

SNOW WHITE

From its opening shot of the wicked queen's castle, to the exquisite shimmering view from underwater of its heroine peering into a well, *Snow White and the Seven Dwarfs* announced that it was something entirely new when it premiered in late 1937. Hailed by one critic as "the most delightful thing ever seen on a screen," the picture was an immediate, runaway success for Walt Disney. The cinematographic techniques used in *Snow White* held their own with the best filmmaking of the era, and the film's lavish animation set a new standard for the craft. More than 60 years later, *Snow White* stands as a cinematic landmark.

In the audience at the film's December 21 premiere at Hollywood's Carthay Circle Theatre were, among others, Clark Gable, Carole Lombard, Lionel Barrymore and Charlie Chaplin. One of the animators on the project, Ward Kimball, remembered, "Clark Gable and Carole Lombard were sitting close, and when Snow White was poisoned, stretched out on that slab, they started blowing their noses. I could hear it—crying—that was the big surprise. We worried about ... whether [audience members] would feel for this girl, and when they did, I knew it was in the bag. Everybody did."

The creators of *Snow White* had reason to be skeptical about the fate of their project. The film was a risky proposition from the outset. Apart from an obscure 1917 Argentine film, *El Apostle*, there had never been a feature-length animated movie, and critics who dubbed the project "Disney's Folly," weren't optimistic about this one. Three months before the film's release animators were still drawing scenes, and the 750 people involved in the project were working 15-hour days. By October, the ink-and-paint and camera crews were working around the clock to add the finishing touches.

Disney had estimated the film would cost $250,000 to produce, and hoped it would gross $1

The fanciful characters and detailed illustration of *Snow White* (left and above) attracted millions of moviegoers in 1938.

91

"If it were customary on this page to rate pictures by the common star or letter system, *Snow White* would have to get six A's, 10 stars, eight bells, a dozen full moons, and three or four Haley's comets."

—*EXCERPT FROM A FILM REVIEW AFTER* SNOW WHITE'S *NATIONAL RELEASE IN FEBRUARY 1938.*

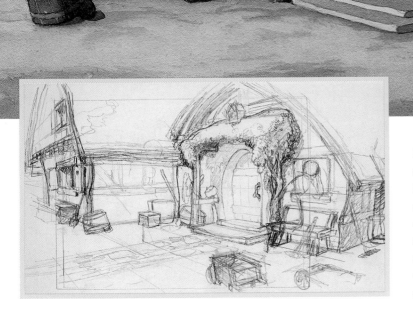

Disney's illustrators (opposite page, above) labored long hours to create his company's first animated classic; the voice for the character of Snow White (opposite page, inset right) was provided by diva Adriana Caselotti (opposite page, inset left); the evil Queen (opposite page, right) was one of Disney's most enduring villains; preceding the final illustrations (above), Disney's animators produced so-called "layout inspiration sketches" (left).

million. He was wrong on both counts. During the five years of production, his original staff of 150 grew five-fold, and in 1937, having already spent more than $1 million on the project, Walt was told by his business-manager brother, Roy, that they would need about $250,000 more to finish the movie. Walt took the unfinished film, fleshed out with animators' rough sketches, to his backers. "I sat alone with Joe Rosenberg of the Bank of America, watching those bits and pieces on a screen," he recalled years later. "He didn't show the slightest reaction to what he'd just seen. He walked out of the projection room, remarked that it was a nice day, and yawned. Then he turned to me and said, 'Walt, that picture will make a pot full of money.'"

In spite of the Depression, the Walt Disney Company had been thriving by producing enormously popular seven-minute cartoon shorts such as *Steamboat Willie* (1928) and *Three Little Pigs* (1933) at the rate of more than one per month. But Walt's soaring creativity and scrupulous attention to storytelling and artistic quality in the production of *Snow White* had turned the film into a make-or-break project for the company. Before it

94

HIS FIRST FULL LENGTH FEATURE PRODUCTION!

Walt DISNEY'S Snow White and the Seven Dwarfs

in the Marvelous MULTIPLANE TECHNICOLOR

©W.D.P.

Before Disney (opposite page, right) finalized his beloved, animated tale of Snow White (opposite page, left) and her quirky friends such as Grumpy (right) and Doc (left), the Disney team developed detailed annotated drawings of all the major characters, including Dopey (opposite page, below); the movie poster (above) trumpeted the film's technicolor charm.

was finished, the budget ballooned to nearly $1.5 million. But, Disney being Disney, this story has a happy ending: The story of the porcelain-skinned princess and her seven little helpers generated an unprecedented $10 million at the box office in 1938. Audiences were thrilled by the dazzling, extraordinarily detailed animation, the hilarious personalities of the Seven Dwarfs and, perhaps most of all, the gripping tale.

The film's success helped transform the Disney name. As Walt said in the early '60s, "I used to be Disney, but now Disney is something we've built up in the public mind....It stands for something, and you don't have to explain what it is."

Especially not to kids—of any age.

Aftermath

Snow White and the Seven Dwarfs is one of the most profitable films of all time, having taken in some $700 million at the box office in nine theatrical releases since its 1937 debut. In 1994, after vowing for years to keep the crown jewel in the vaults, Disney released *Snow White* on video, in which format it has of course been an enormous success.

In 1939 The National Academy of Motion Picture Arts and Scientists gave the Disney studio a Special Oscar for *Snow White*. At that year's Academy Awards ceremonies, 10-year-old Shirley Temple presented Walt with eight statuettes: one big Oscar and seven little ones.

INDEX